Chef Terri Rogers is a self-taught chef/serial entrepreneur in the food and beverage industry. She is the founder and CEO of *NOoodle*, a healthy plant-based made in the USA food startup company. She has been selling her *NOoodle* products on TV via QVC/HSN and select retailers and food service establishments for over ten years. As a previous restauranteur in the suburbs of Chicago, she catered to high profile clients, including the guests of *The Oprah Winfrey* show. Her books detail what it really takes to be a 'David' in our world of Goliath's in one of the only essential businesses left in our world today...the business of food. As an empathic leader in the future of food, *March Forth in Love,* is her blueprint to a bigger and better America for all Americans. Her book which exposes grave truths in our society today, creates a plan to extend the last harvest predicted to be 2080 to...infinity and beyond.

My book is dedicated to my sons, Alex, and Jake, two empath leaders of GENamaZing.

My book is dedicated to all the future empath leaders of GENamaZing, a.k.a. GEN Z.

My book is dedicated to all the women I met who are currently incarcerated and drugged against their will in mental institutions throughout our country.

My book is dedicated to all the children and adults in our country and throughout the world who are homeless.

My book is dedicated to all the entrepreneurs who believe they are sitting on the next true unicorn…sitting on it doesn't do it any good…it's about putting your idea into action over a long period of time.

Chef Terri Rogers

MARCH FORTH IN LOVE

AUSTIN MACAULEY PUBLISHERS™

LONDON · CAMBRIDGE · NEW YORK · SHARJAH

Ordering Information
Quantity sales: Special discounts are available on quantity purchases by corporations, associations, and others. For details, contact the publisher at the address below.

Publisher's Cataloging-in-Publication data
Rogers, Chef Terri
March Forth in Love

ISBN 9781649798725 (Paperback)
ISBN 9781649798732 (Hardback)
ISBN 9781649798756 (ePub e-book)
ISBN 9781649798749 (Audiobook)

Library of Congress Control Number: 2022903419

www.austinmacauley.com/us

First Published 2022
Austin Macauley Publishers LLC
40 Wall Street, 33rd Floor, Suite 3302
New York, NY 10005
USA

mail-usa@austinmacauley.com
+1 (646) 5125767

"You have to keep breaking your heart until it opens."

– Rumi

Thank you to the many people who have crossed my path in life. You all have inspired my life in a profoundly positive way. Thank you to my brand ambassadors and loyal customers. Without you, I would have thrown in the towel at least a hundred times. Most importantly, I wouldn't have had the chance to write this book for U.S. Today, my heart is wide open, *te amo*.

Chapter 1

The Last Harvest Is Predicted
to be 2080? WTF?

It was February 28th, 2020. I had been suffering in my tiny 370-square-foot garden apartment on the UWS with my allergies flaring up for months now. I was completely out of my prescribed meds, montelukast also known as singular. They usually prescribe it for kids with asthma, but it also helps with different pathogens of allergies. I am extremely sensitive to all drugs and luckily for me, my allergist in 2013 assured me singular had no side effects. "We give it to young children," I remember her telling me.

ON March 4, 2020 the FDA issued a new safety announcement about montelukast (Singular), a popular drug used by people with asthma and seasonal allergies. The FDA decided to add a new black box warning to this medication, the most prominent warning it can impose. This is due to serious mental health side effects associated with this drug.

As allergy season comes into full swing, people with allergies or asthma may be restarting this medication or already taking it. If you are, speak with your healthcare provider to fully understand the risks and benefits associated with this medication, especially if you have pre-existing mental health problems like depression or anxiety.

Here's what you need to know about the warning.

What is montelukast for?

Montelukast is used to prevent and treat asthma in children and adults. It is also used to relieve symptoms of allergic rhinitis. It works by blocking the effects of leukotrienes, which cause your airways to narrow or swell.

The FDA approved the brand version, Singular, in 1998. The generic, montelukast, has been available since 2012.

What prompted the FDA's decision?

This isn't the first time the FDA has investigated the link between montelukast and mental health side effects. In 2008, manufacturer Merck updated the drug labeling four times to account for reported side effects of tremors, anxiousness, depression, and suicide. During this time, the FDA asked Merck to conduct more studies on the link between the drug and suicidal behavior.

Recently, the FDA re-evaluated the drug's risks based on reports of suicide and other harmful side effects submitted to its Adverse Event Reporting System (FAERS). Based on this reassessment, the FDA decided to issue the warning. Montelukast was known to have mental health side effects, but many health providers weren't aware of how serious they were.

What are the health risks associated with this medication?

The following side effects were reported in patients who used montelukast:

- Agitation
- Depression
- Sleeping problems
- Suicidal thoughts and actions

I also didn't have any epi-pens in my possession that were not expired. EpiPen's are the only thing that can save my life if I was to have another full out anaphylaxis attack.

I knew I had to go to the doctor, but I was lazy. I needed all new doctors. I was a new NYC resident, and I didn't have any set up yet. The dry heat from my base heater was always pushing out so much dry heat and making my allergies worse. For me, to be able to breathe I needed to keep my sub ground windows wide open in the middle of winter. I had requested several times from my building management to lower the heat in my unit. They told me there was nothing they could do. It was an old brownstone, one system for the entire building.

I was working on documents I needed to submit to Food Future Co. *NOoodle* was just invited to their accelerated program for healthy food startup companies. Shen Tong was the billionaire who owned Food future co. His program was set to begin on April 1st. I had to quickly turn my LLC into a C-corporation if I wanted to be part of his program. After several rounds/call backs/interviews *NOoodle* won a spot. Shen Tong told me they had over 600 companies apply to the program. My company was one of eight to make the spring 2020 program.

Suddenly, I remember feeling as if something was in my eye. Unconsciously I started rubbing my eyes. I started having the tingling sensation that comes on prior to my body going panic and starts to swell up. I looked in the mirror and sure enough both my eyes looked like I just got punched in the face. I stopped touching my face instantly. I knew I couldn't scratch, stretching and rubbing my itch could kill me. What happens first is the outsides start swelling up and then your insides swell up and block your ability to breathe. It is extremely life threatening as I have learned from my past attacks, they can be a life-or-death situation for me. The more attacks I have, the quicker my lungs completely close. I pooped two Benadryl and ran as fast as I could to the urgent care center. Luckily for me, it was right around the block on Columbus Ave. I had previously scoped it out. The office manager took one look at me and quickly escorted me back to see a doctor.

The urgent care doctor was adorable, young-looking and a very pregnant woman. I had explained to her my history since January 2013 when I first had an anaphylaxis attack. She said, "I don't think the singular with Benadryl is enough to prevent these flare-ups." She told me she recommends something stronger, prednisone.

I said, "Steroids for allergy attacks?"

She said, "Yes, they are much stronger which is what I believe you need; something stronger."

She prescribed me a refill on my singular, two new EpiPen's and Prednisone. I went directly across to the

Duane Reade, and they quickly filled my scripts. I went back home, took my medications, and got back to work.

Prior to accepting the invitation to Food Future CO accelerated program, I did some research on my new partner. It was something I learned to do over the course of my career, google everyone. Partners in business can be as crippling as a bad partner in marriage. Sometimes business partners can even be harder to break. The only two ways I know how to get rid of business partners is to buy them out or if your company goes belly up. In business, no one wants to go bankrupt, a terrible partner is better than going bankrupt. I can compare it to life and death. Life is the game and when we die, the game is over. Owning a company is the game and when the company goes bankrupt, the game is over too. I want to always play the game, always. If only we could all live forever, but that is just not life. I think the hardest concept to live with is the fact that we all die, game over.

I watched every interview on Shen Tong I could find. I saw one negative situation with his wife in the news. I didn't pay it much attention. After all, what male and/or female in our world is perfect? None of us are! I have learned to pay attention to the sum of the accomplishments over time. We can never judge one person for something that happened once. As humans we must be compassionate of others. I believe to do so we must try to look at the negative situation as a 'mis-step' in a lifetime of greatness.

I was so impressed with Shen Tong after I met him for the first time. Talk about a humble genius, he certainly was this to me and I was in awe of his accomplishments thus far. If you google him, it says the following: Shen Tong is an

American impact investor, activist, and writer. He founded business accelerators Food Future Co in 2015 and Food-X in 2014, the latter or which is recognized by Fast Company as one of "the world's topmost innovative companies of 2015 in food." He was a Chinese dissident who was exiled as one of the student leaders in the democracy movement in Tiananmen Square in 1989. He studied at Boston University and Harvard University.

I stumbled first on his Ted Talk from 2015 called *feeding the movement*. These are some of my favorite takeaways:

Shen says, "Food is a problem of failed market mechanisms. Food is a global epidemic. A perfect storm may happen. Not only can we change the world for good, but I will make the argument and I hope some of you will follow us. Those who really focus on the best solutions in terms of impact on people and on the planet will be the food innovations that are the most profitable. But more than anything else, it is a cultural change. There is a better way we nurture our body and our community and preserve nature and the environment. Shoppers are starting to ask the questions, where is my food coming from? More than 90% of our food choices are being made, highly processed and we don't even know where our food comes from. Each time we buy, we cook, we offer food, that is a vote. That is a direct democracy vote. A function of democracy does not depend only on the right to vote. It is equally dependent on the concentration of viable alternatives. This is where I see this huge opportunity. This opportunity is not only for profit but also for people's social impact and for the planet. The opportunity is to restore the efficiency that is almost naturally there. We have this wealth of systems that has been tested even before mankind existed, it is called *nature*. We believe if we really focus on the big picture and doing good. Our brains do not need to be tricked when it comes to food.

"Real food is naturally satisfying, and our brains know that. Nature is our friend, that is the real friend here. So, this is one movement…a long-term movement…that I have joined where I can have a smile on my face. Not because food unites, it rarely divides. it is because this is a movement as profound as it is, I can see the finish line. And mark my words and I have gone thru some tough shit, problems, pardon my Chinese (lol). That was a chicken out of the cave. Its hand holding real innovators and joining forces with policy changes, protests, and cultural changes so that together, together, we can regain that respect of nature that gave birth to mankind. Together we are going to do good and do very well. And you know what? This time while we are doing good, the good dead is not the reward itself…it is better. I am not talking about profit because when nature is recognized and respected and the resilience is restored and we leverage it, it will reward us handsomely and make this a delicious movement. Thank you."

A year ago, he spoke in Manhattan on Sustainable food. The interview only got 352 views. *What a shame*, I thought. No wonder our world seems doomed. Our leaders are not having the correct conversations they need to be having.

I will paraphrase Shen again:

"The reason I am here is because I have three young children who live in NYC. It is hard to feed them clean food. There is a tremendous problem which also creates a huge opportunity. Agriculture is not just our health, or the taste, and the environment but essential to society, humankind, and this planet. Fortunately, what I realized about ten years ago, we are in a better situation in changing food because millennials led this shift demanding healthier and traceable foods. Millennials made food the new black, they made it fashionable. This gave change makers good solutions. We don't have to protest or preach or even change policies, that would be nice and great to see but we can build scalable businesses that would make the current situation obsolete. We don't have a shortage of food. We have an oversupply of empty calories filled with chemicals and negligible. In terms of balancing impact vs. making money. The opportunity in value creation is in the impact. The most interesting thing we have learned in the last five years is not as much tech but more so the actual holistic understanding of water and soil. It is a trend that is great for us, for our planet and for our children. I remember this one moment, the smartest people gathered in Silicon Valley. I had this conversation with a legendary founder of a major US technology company. I said, 'Look…if I had system 'A' that is the height of science and technology and system 'B' the highest ecological, biological and cultural. Which of the two systems is smarter? He said, 'Of course, Shen, Biological/Ecological wins."

"I said, 'I rest my case.' We must return to the understanding of biodiversity and the resilience of nature, our forests, our oceans, our rivers. In healthy soil, we have rich and smart systems that are in nature. The Buddhists have done this for a couple of thousand years, they have done something right. All we must do is not to play God anymore. We can use science and technology to leverage resilience of those two complex systems. We can recover what we destroyed in the last half century in no time *(applaud from the audience)*. 99.5% of the meat in the US, I wouldn't feed my children, if I care about their health. This is not a fad; it is a major multi-faceted shift. It is here to stay. If you follow the disruptive model, the time frame of the future I would say anywhere between 20 and 50 years the change would happen. But at the same time, do we have twenty years?

"Plant based food agriculture has twice the impact on the environment. It is not as mainstream yet in terms of policy change. Right now, we are at 25% of clean energy in the world in the work we started twenty years which is a great effort. We should applaud that right? *(Audience applauds)*. Which also means seventy-five percent is still bad. I am not even sure how many elections around the world make food part of their platform? We are kind of behind in the eleventh hour. We may not even have time. We may not have earth to work with. So, there is a real urgency. Hopefully, this behavior shift will be the real tidal wave to carry this forward."

The commentator states, "It is easy to sound like an alarmist. Yes, we are running out of time. I believe we have sixty years left of soil, right Shen?"

Shen Tong says, "Yes, sixty harvests left on Earth."

The commentator adds, "We won't be able to grow food anymore because the soil will not have enough nutritional density to actually grow food."

Shen says, "Yes…but the good news is that nature is so resilient, if we just give it a chance for the Earth to go back into our guts and go back into the soil…back into the oceans and waters, nature will just recover itself very quickly. There is a silver lining to that. Food is absolutely the most direct democracy. Where you put your dollar is the most important. Find the local farmers markets. Grow your own food, even a little bit. As soon as you touch food and grow food, ninety percent of the problem will be gone."

Did he/they just say the last harvest is predicted to be 2080? WTF? Alex and Jake will only be 83 and 81 years young. What about their children, my future grandchildren? Is this true? Does this mean my future grandchildren are going to starve to death before they hit their fiftieth birthday? OMG, this is the worst news I have ever heard! Oh no, this can't be true! We must stop this from happening! How do we stop this from happening?

Chapter 2

I Saw the Bats in Hubei, China

I woke up the next day and my allergies were gone. I was inhaling and exhaling without any complications. I couldn't believe how fast the new meds worked. *Why didn't my allergy specialist in Chicago ever prescribe me steroids?* I wondered.

The information I found out from researching Shen Tong (regarding the future of food) was bothering me. I couldn't concentrate on anything else. I started googling and reading more published articles on the last harvest. I wanted to know if Shen Tong was correct. I knew in my gut Shen Tong was telling the truth. I wish I didn't know what I knew today. Today I wished I was not a philomath. The saying, 'Ignorance is bliss' came to mind. I never really believed ignorance was bliss. Now I understand, I get it. I thought I would be happier if I didn't know what I knew today. What happened to the formula, knowledge = power? I don't feel powerful anymore, for the first time in my life I feel powerless.

I started thinking about the Coronavirus. It was so odd for me to know that Covid-19 originated in Hubei Province, China. I spent time in 2013 in Hubei, China. Right after I received a $500,000 LOI for *NOoodle* from Mr. Wonderful (O'Leary Ventures from my Shark Tank experience), they thought it would be a great idea to go to find other sources for the Konjac plant. You can have a billion-dollar idea but if you don't have the supply chain locked up, it may be smarter to call it quits before you lose all your money. Take it from someone like me who learned this the hard way with *NOoodle*. I flew with my boyfriend at the time to Shanghai. He got D-1 status when he got divorced because his ex-wife was a flight attendant for American Airlines. D-1 status means you can basically fly anywhere in the world, provided there are seats for a very small fee in comparison to what it would normally cost if you didn't have D-1 status. We flew business class there and first-class back. It cost my company a total of $818 for two tickets from Chicago to Shanghai. What a bargain! I was more excited about flying to China in luxury than I was to be in China. China was never on my bucket list. I never desired to go, the idea of visiting a communist country was a bit scary to me. Regarding many things China in my mind was and still is a third world country. It was mid-august, and I never experienced humid heat like the kind I experienced in Hubei in 2013.

We checked into Hyatt on the Bund; it was amazing! Wow! What a hotel and a view from the top was incredible. The buffet brunch in the hotel was the best I have ever had. The choices, OMG. It was five countries buffets all at once. I was blessed to eat this buffet three times while we were in China. Each time we stayed for at least two hours eating and I am not exaggerating. They had all the American choices a five-star hotel would have, i.e., smoked salmon, bagels, made to order omelets, pancakes, fresh toast, toast, eggs benedict, and all the sweets to go all with it. They also had all the choices you would see at a breakfast buffet in England. You know, the proper English breakfast that includes lots of bacon and sausage, grilled tomatoes, sauteed button mushrooms, beans of some kind, and of course, some rendition of tater tots. It included all French and Italian pastries, cured meat and cheeses galore. In addition, they had so many different varieties of dim sum which is my favorite! Omg…I was in heaven.

After a couple of nights in Shanghai we took a two-hour flight to Hubei. The service was very similar to what we find here in the states on United or American airlines. Instead of alcohol, everyone got hot tea and a juice box. We arrived in Hubei and waited in the airport for our Chinese hosts. Employees of a company called Hubei Yizhi Konjac Biotechnology Co, Ltd., who invited us to China when we applied for our Chinese visas. They farm and produce the Konjac yam powder. They picked us up and drove us to the factory. We were their guests in the hotel that was designed for factory guests like us only. Cindy, who was our bi-lingual host, told us there were no real hotels in this province. The factory and the hotel were behind an electric fence with barbed wire around the top.

The 'hotel' they had was complimentary, they paid for all our expenses during our visit in Hubei. It only had five rooms; it was an extension of the factory. It was nice and clean and modern. It also had air conditioning and a great view of the landscaped mountains.

It was a surreal experience from start to finish. I remember the first night they took us to dinner. We took a boat across the Yangtze River to get to the small restaurant. There were only two private rooms, a small kitchen and a door that led to the bathroom. Cindy told us this was a very special restaurant, and the food was special. We were five in total, and we all sat down on the ground with a table that was about two feet off the ground. I was so hot, there was no air conditioning. The food was hot both in a warm way and in a very spicy way. I love spicy food but this…wow. I was dripping sweat the entire time. The food was delicious! We were eating things that I never ate before i.e., pigs' feet. I didn't want to insult my quests, so I tried everything. We each were given our own set of chopsticks and the different large sharing plates started to come out, so many different plates for sharing. It all looked amazing, and I love that about Chinese food; so many different choices in one meal. The problem was there were no serving spoons or forks. The table would move, like a big poo-poo platter. We all would take our chopsticks and pick up our food from the large plates and bring the food over to our individual small plates. I couldn't get over the amount of double dipping we were doing. I was so grossed out but as the saying goes, "When in Rome…"

One thing they never seemed to have been ice. Even when we landed in Shanghai, I noticed all the water fountains in the airport had warm water and not cold. The only cold thing I could find to drink was cold beer, so in China, beer was my go-to. After dinner I went to use the bathroom, it was a hole in the ground. Not a port, a potty, an actual hole in the ground. After dinner, Cindy asked us if we wanted to join the party in the next room. They were a group of six Chinese officials. We played cards with them, and we watched these men get very drunk on the Chinese wine. If you have not had Chinese wine before, I would say to skip it. It is very different from any other wine I have ever had. I couldn't believe that I was at a card game with some of the Chinese government in the middle of mainland China. What are the odds?

The next day we got up and we had breakfast on the streets. I remember seeing the raw chickens, what looked like bats and many eggs sitting out in the hot sun. Cindy asks me what I want to have for breakfast. My choices were hot spicy soup or eggs, or chicken with ramen. I was so hot and dripping sweat. I didn't want hot tea or hot spicy soup or eggs that have been sitting out in the sun. She asked me, "Would you like some hot tea?"

I said, "No, thank you, do you have a bottle of water?" Cindy instructed the boss man to get John and I two bottles of water. They were room temperature. John loved his hot and sour soup. It looked good but between the heat of it and the fact that all this food has been sitting out without refrigeration I politely passed. We drove about an hour and half into the mountains to one of the plantations they owned that grew the Konjac Yam. We toured the plantation. It seemed very unorganized. I was walking over fences and hoses, not like a typical farm/plantation I have seen here in the states. There was one barn with lots of seeds on the ground with bugs and flies all around. I didn't seem sanitary to me. Besides the Hyatt on the Bund, where we stayed in Shanghai, I didn't feel comfortable eating anything. I owned restaurants for years prior. I understood how easily we can get sick from eating some foods that have been sitting out in the hot sun. If you ever have had food poisoning you know it is not something you want to get, especially not in mainland China.

After the plantation field trip, we toured the factory that turns the root of the Konjac plant, the corm, into potato fiber flour. It was very interesting, and I enjoyed the detailed tour. They took us to another amazing restaurant for lunch and then for dinner. By this time, I was used to sharing germs with my hosts. The next day they drove us back to the airport to return to Shanghai.

In Shanghai, we toured another factory, this was a factory that produced the finished noodles. Our host was amazing. His factory, about an hour drive out of Shanghai, was not so amazing. Open windows to the outside, puddles of water on the inside. Bugs and farm animals running all over the place. On the property there was a small building with lots of windows and clothes hanging outside. I noticed several men sticking their heads out with no shirt on, clearly this building had no air conditioning either. Our host told us this was where his factory workers live. It was a sight for sore eyes. After our factory tour he drove us to his house, we picked up his two young kids and wife and we went to an old famous water town called Zhou Zhuang. It was very old with small bridges and canals. Our host told us it was one of the oldest towns in Shanghai. He then picked a place for us to have lunch. I noticed, except for Hyatt on the bund, it was hard to find an alcoholic drink. The only people I saw drinking were those government officials that night in Hubei. At lunch, we had cokes and orange sodas and our host ordered a lot of different plates of food. The little fried fish came first. Our host says to us with a big smile, "These fish came right out of the river." We had a big window that looked out on this little river which looked to me like the color of mud. I whispered to John, "I am not eating those fish. I won't do it."

After our trip, I reported back to my future partners at O'Leary ventures that I would never make the *NOoodle* in China, no way! In fact, if I could help it, I wouldn't be going back to China ever again. The people were nice, but I felt extremely lucky that I didn't catch a foodborne illness. If ever did have to go back for business, it would *not* be in the middle of August.

I experienced first-hand how exactly this pandemic came to be, from the source, the root of Covid-19. The virus became a reality of the exact fear I had seven years prior when I was there. The idea that my biggest competitor, Miracle noodle, is now selling millions and millions and millions of noodles made from 97% water, water from China has concerned me for years. I knew most of our food sources were not controlled because it was mostly imported from other countries. How can our institutions, i.e., the FDA and USDA inspect these plantations and factories properly? These people sit at their desks, they don't travel the world of factories. It's a total joke from my POV. The FDA is concerned with serving sizes, ha! *Lol*, it seems unimportant to me since everyone usually does what they want to do. They eat what they want to eat. How many times have you eaten a whole bag of Lays potato chips (maybe 15 servings) by yourself in your life? I rest my case. I wondered why people are eating noodles made from 97% water from China. They must not know. How could they know? They hide the origin effectively. It is distributed in Miami on the front and then tucked away on the back it says, Made in

China. 'We' as a group of American citizens really pay no attention to where our food sources are made. We believe they are made in America usually unless they are a special cheese from France or Caviar from Russia, etc.

The Fancy Food show is a perfect example of the hypocrisy that exists in the food business today. The Fancy Food Show, for those of you who have never heard of it, is the largest specialty food show in the world. It happens two times per year. Once in January in San Francisco and once in June in NYC at the Jacob Javits center. *NOoodle* has been an exhibit at both locations. I have also walked the Fancy Food Show as a guest approximately 20 times over the course of my career. Many countries have aisles of booths, however, most companies who exist at this show are American owned companies. Naturally as consumers we would assume most of the American companies were manufacturing most of their products here in the USA. This is false. Most of our food sources today are imported from other countries. I see this as a great opportunity to create millions and millions of new jobs here at home, plant based made in the USA foods is essential to extending the last harvest from 2080 to…

"Infinity and beyond!" – Buzz lightyear.

Chapter 3

An Idiopathic Nightmare Begins

It is Sunday, March 1st, and I was preparing for my birthday party. One of my favorite quotes by the Dave Matthews Band. "Celebrate and do it well, because life is short but sweet for certain." A seasoned party planner, I love hosting parties. My birthday party was going to be at one of my favorite clubs in NYC. It is called the Sugar Bar. It is Ashford and Simpsons place, remember them? It was going to be awesome because on Wednesday nights they had the most amazing band playing my favorite music, Motown music. I loved the southern food they served there too. It was going to be an intimate party, I had 13 people confirmed for dinner and fun. On the menu, yum…fried chicken, collard greens, mashed potatoes, and corn bread. I was planning to make black and white cupcakes to bring in for dessert. The manager was going to decorate and get lots and lots of balloons.

I was planning on singing one of my favorite songs (with the band as my backup) by my childhood mentor, Stevie Wonder, "Happy Birthday." It is a song he wrote for Martin Luther King, and I know every word by heart. It was Stevie and Kunta Kinte and Stephanie mills who were my original mentors growing up. My mom made our family watch the special, "Roots." I was eight at the time, my sister, twelve, and my brother, six years old. I will never forget the details of that movie that changed my life. I guess I was always an empathic person maybe because I was born that way. I was blessed because I was raised with the arts and my mom exposed me to everything growing up. Nothing came as a surprise, and I liked it that way. She made me take Werner Erhard EST training in NYC when I was eight years old. She dragged us with her when she stood online for hours to buy John Denver tickets. She took to Broadway shows like "The Wiz" and "Jesus Christ Superstar" and movies like, "Hair." We were raised with all holidays *except* for Easter. My mom was adamant that although Jesus Christ was a person there's absolutely no proof that he rose from the dead. I remember when I asked her at a young age, we were outside. I said, "Mom…what happens when we die?"

She said, "You come back in a different form, you could be a cat in your next life, or a tree or a bird."

I remember it was not very inspiring to know I would be a cat. I wanted to be me. I wanted to be me forever. I remember years later when I was thirty. I was having dinner at a famous restaurant called Mr. Chow. Mr. Chow, growing up, was my dad's favorite and he would take us there on special occasions. Besides the amazing green prawns, Chicken Satay, Peking Duck, fried seaweed and crispy beef and lychee nuts. Mr. Chow always seemed to have famous people dining there. I was never one to really care about meeting famous people. I lived in the Silk building, on top of Tower Records in Greenwich Village growing up. Cher lived there too, along with Keith Richards and Patti Hanson.

I would go to popular clubs as a teenager including the famous Nel's, Limelight and the Tunnel. Sharing cocktails with stars like Jagger, Eddie Murphy, Prince, Princess Stephanie, Michel Baryshnikov, etc., etc. I was used to meeting stars and that was cool.

It wasn't until I met my true idol growing up, Stevie Wonder, that I knew I had to interrupt his dinner with his wife. I had to tell him the positive impact he has made on my life. Before I could stop myself, I went up to his table and I said, "Hi, Stevie…my name is Terri, and I am your biggest fan!"

He said, "Hi, Terri, say hi to my wife."

I said, "Hi! Can I sing you guys a song that has inspired my life in a huge positive way since I was a young teen?"

He said, "Sure." I started singing right then and there at Mr. Chows. Standing up at his table while he and his wife were sitting down.

I sang, "You just could not know how long we tried, to see how this building looked inside."

Stevie looked up at me and smiled and said, "Wow…you know that one!"

I continued to sing. "This must be a lucky day for me. Because the sign says there's a vacancy." Then in another voice I sang, "Look, I know you came a long way, but you made it just too late. So, we had to give it to somebody else." Then I sang the other man's part, "Well, I talked to you on the phone less than fifteen minutes ago and you told me that it was cool I graduated from Harvard U. My job pays good money too, and if you check on my resume, you'll find they all wanted me to stay." My other voice sings, "Well I can't take the time out to check your credit card cause the computer just broke down today." Then my other voice sings, "Well, I'll stop by here tomorrow to complete your interview, but I know what you are going to say. I know your bottom line is…you might have the cash, but you cannot cash in your face…we don't want your kind living here." I stopped after the chorus. I wanted to sing the whole song, but I knew I was interrupting his time with his wife. I said my goodbyes. Maybe one day I will get to sing the whole song for him, maybe even with him.

As James Dean said, "Dream as you will live forever, live as you will die today."

I had started a blog a couple of years ago on LinkedIn called, "How to create a sustainable plant-based food startup." I was on rule number 171 and had 4700 followers. On someone's feed, people were complaining about one of the largest specialty food trade shows in the country known as, "The All-Natural Expo West," not canceling the show due to COVID. At that point, they did not cancel the show and were not going to refund any companies money. The big healthy food brands, i.e., Kind Bar, were speaking up on behalf of all the smaller healthy food brands which I thought was cool. Leaders need to lead especially in times of trouble. Of course, they had decided as a company not to go. They obviously wanted a full refund and/or credit to a future show. It was prudent to cancel for the general safety of the public. In the meantime, it was Sunday, and I started commenting and speaking my objective truths of what I know regarding the integrity of the food business in our country today.

New HOPE was UNFI's marketing arm. UNFI is the largest specialty food distributor in the country. UNFI a few years back, after Jeff Bezos bought Whole Foods, became the exclusive specialty food distributor to Whole Foods stores nationwide. Whole foods, most people know, are owned today by Amazon. I started speaking out against the largest monopoly in the food business the world has ever seen. A spider monopoly that crosses the vertical and horizontal planes at once. Jeff Bezos is creator and owner of this amazing spider monopoly.

UNFI was like our current president in my mind. A big bully who had all the power A big bully that hurt the little people/companies and helped the bigger people/companies. NOoodle just received a bunch of chargebacks from them last week on the most recent check they sent. This was UNFI's way of doing business with small food brands. At the end of every calendar year, without fail, they would create some phony charge backs on freight, on confusing invoices, anything they could find to take my companies' profits. It is well known in the food industry that UNFI puts *many* small startup food companies out of business this way. They have been doing this ever since *NOoodle* started working with them back in2010. Not to mention my supply manager was a big bully from my POV. I hated working with her. She was a total bitch to people like me who owned small food companies. My company couldn't afford to support her/UNFI's quarterly advertising fees. When I did advertise with them NOoodle never saw any increase in sales big enough that would pay for these extra fees they demand from all of their vendors. Even without the advertising fees, UNFI was taking all my profit out with these chargebacks year after year. I had distribution in over 100 Wholefoods and over 100 Wegmans but the

31

chargebacks and the stress it was causing me knowing they were able to do this wasn't worth it. If I wanted to work with them, I had no say in the matter. Her name is Ginger Lynch. I always thought it was ironic her name ended with the word, "Lynch."

The next day I woke up feeling so powerful It was hard to explain, invincible with tons of energy. I called my dad, who was always in my memory big into the stock market. I requested him to sell all his stocks. I said, "Dad! You must sell all your stocks right now! You must get out of the stock market. It is going to crash and crash big!"

He said, "Terri...why are you talking crazy again? You have no idea what you are talking about!"

I said, "I do...I know it is going to crash. I know this because of what I know regarding the future of food."

He said, "Please...Terri...don't upset me like this, goodnight."

That night I woke up from thoughts in my head that I was going to die. I didn't sleep a wink. I cried all night long. I was scared to death. The next morning, I received a call from my supply manager, Ginger Lynch. She never called me...ever. Every interaction for years was via email. She would never pick up any of my phone calls. I knew it was her because my phone said, Providence, Rhode Island. UNFI headquarters were in Providence, and it was the only contact I had in that city. She said, "Terri, we saw your posts on LinkedIn and you're out!"

I said, "Go fuck yourself, cunt!" and hung up the phone. I have never in my life said that word out loud until that day. It was unlike me but when I hung up the phone I felt as if I was on top of the world. I finally took a stand for myself, finally after all these years. I wasn't going to be manipulated anymore. Just because they had all the power, they were never playing fair from my POV.

My father called about thirty minutes after I hung up on Ginger and he said, "Terri…I have no idea why or how you knew the market was going to crash, but you were right! Did you see the market today? The market is crashing, and it is crashing big!"

I said, "I didn't look at it today. I told you what was going to happen, but you didn't listen."

He was amazed that I called the crash. Anyway, we said our goodbyes and I hung up. I had so much energy at 7:00 pm. I decided to go for a run in Central Park. I never run; I am not a runner. After my double-bunionectomy bouncing on my feet is not the best form of exercise. I also made a rule as a teenager never to go into Central Park at night by myself. I had to go to the Sugar bar to go over the last-minute details and pay the balance that was due on my party. It was raining out and so I started running very fast. I remember thinking I was Forrest Gump and I said to myself, "Run, Forest, Run!" I was wearing my home alert necklace that I started to wear ever since my last anaphylaxis attack. It is hard for me to remember what happened next. I just remember for some reason, I couldn't breathe, probably because I was running so fast.

I woke up at Mt. Sinai on the upper east side the next night at 11:00 pm, March 4th, 2020. My birthday would be over in an hour. What happened to me over the last 24 hours plus? I was so confused. I had no idea what happened to me. I remember falling and hitting the emergency button on my necklace in Central Park. I remember ER techs pinching and prodding. I remember a bunch of faces, maybe six staring at me and laughing.

They gave me a white bread tuna sandwich and my dirty clothes, a little bottle of Apple Juice and my release papers. I left the hospital in a dry muddy outfit. My backpack was gone with all my things. In my vest pocket, I had fifteen dollars. I took a taxi to my best friend's house, Candy Kole because I didn't have a phone or keys to get into my apartment. Candy and I have been best friends since fifth grade. We traveled to Europe together for two summers when we were 19 and 21 years young. I paid for my trips 100% from the money I made from my clothing business back then. She paid for her trip 100% by asking her dad. It was the typical behavior of many of the parents of my childhood friends. The first thing (in my memory) my father ever taught me besides skiing was the value of a dollar. I loved working for every dollar he helped me earn as a child. Candy now is a self-made kid-less multi-millionaire. She gave me a blanket and I slept on the couch. In the morning, she woke me up and told me Miles (her husband) was going to drive me home. She had to leave to work. She HAD to leave to work although she is the owner/CEO of her company. We all have priorities and Candy certainly had hers. She looked at me and she said, "Terri please get some help." I looked back at her so completely dazed and confused and then she was gone.

What happened to me? When I went home, I found my door was broken into by the fire department at 2:00 am in the morning. My emergency necklace sent them to my house instead of where I was (which is not what the necklace is designed to do). They are designed to send the medical help to where we are to save us from dying for an anaphylaxis attack. I called a locksmith and had them make new locks. It was March 5th, and I was supposed to fly to W PB airport for my niece's bat mitzvah in three hours. On the way to the airport, I was getting all sorts of texts from my family urging me not to come. My emergency necklace contacted my sister, my son, and my best friend Candy. They all told me to get some help and get a brain scan right away. My family also planned a surprise 80th birthday party the Sunday night following the bat mitzvah. I had several texts from my sister, my sister-in-law Daisy, and my brother all requesting me not to come. I was already in the cab on the way to the airport. I thought about turning around. I really was not in the mood to go to a $100,000 plus party in Boca Raton and hang around all the Jappy girls and their Jappy moms. If you're not aware, the slang word Jappy is the made-up adjective to describe a JAP (Jewish American Princess). Then I thought about my dad. I would never miss my dad's 80th surprise birthday party. If I did, I knew I would regret it.

My kids were flying in from college for the events. I already spent a fortune on our flights and hotels. I missed my kids and I wanted to see them. No…I was going. I flew to Florida knowing no one wanted me around. I even got disinvited to the Friday night party for family and out of towners. I stayed in my hotel…alone. I felt so scared, confused, unwanted and unloved. My kids flew in the next night and when they got to the hotel, they seemed to be the only ones who were concerned for my well-being. They requested for me to get off Facebook. I said, not. I have a right to speak my mind. I choose honesty over acceptance.

At the same time, I was going off on LinkedIn I was going off on Facebook too. Saying things like our president needs to be exiled to Russia and eat potatoes for the rest of his life. I was posting videos of sugar cereals I believe have a huge part in children's diabetes. Videos of me shopping in supermarkets proving almost everything on the market was not made in the USA. My brain seemed to not be able to rest and I wasn't sleeping. I was scared to go to sleep, scared to close my eyes.

On Saturday in Boca, I took Jake to get new glasses and contact lenses. I needed new glasses too. Len's Crafters took us both in at the same time. They took pictures of our eyes and then the doctor showed the pictures of what the insides of our eyes look like through a microscope. It was so cool. Jake's eyes looked like lots of thin white lines going every direction on a dark background. The picture of my eyes on the other hand looked like the most amazing fireworks display. It had so many blasts of colors. We both were amazed, and the doctor agreed it was cool. I guess that is what happens when you're blessed to have undergone five eye surgeries and have both your eyes lasered 360 degrees. I say blessed because many people who have had both their retinas detach unknowingly are blind today.

I flew back to NYC and got back to work. I had to fly to Tampa a few days later to be on HSN with *NOoodle*. I was staying at the Hyatt Hotel in Clearwater Florida. I watched as Florida closed the beach, *this was getting serious*, I thought. I still couldn't fall asleep. I wasn't sure if I couldn't fall asleep or was afraid to fall asleep, it was both.

I went for a walk in Central Park Friday afternoon, March 20th. When I came back to my apartment, I was without a phone, this was the second phone I lost in a month. Not like me at all. I remember making Jerk chicken that night and watching Governor Cuomo on the news by myself. I was totally turned off equally by both the Governor and my chicken. I felt like he was talking to me as if I was in fifth grade. My chicken seemed puffed up with GMO's, I threw it all out and turned off my TV. I was not myself. It was the scariest time of my life. Although my breathing was good, I still thought I was going to die from an anaphylaxis attack or Covid-19. The streets of NYC were desolate. I was so scared to be alone in my dry heated apartment, I was starting to hear voices in my head.

I decided to get out of my apartment and check into the Arlo Hotel in Soho. I figured if something happened to me, I wouldn't be alone, and it was safer for me to be around people. I took $3000 out of my Chase account in the form of $100 bills and took a cab to the hotel. I tipped the driver $100; he was thrilled, and I was thrilled that he was thrilled. All the room service was delivered in plastic cups and containers due to Covid. I stayed in my room for the next several days. I would give each waitress $100 tip when they came to my door to serve my food. I felt so bad for all the people who were working there, they must be scared. If I am scared, they must be too. Not to mention no one was in the hotel so they were not able to make tips with no one there. I figured I would help them by tipping them all tremendously.

I rented so many movies. I watched *1917* and thought the main character at the end was my Irish grandfather that

I never met. I saw "Mr. Rogers" and thought the character Lloyd was based on my ex-husband Lloyd and insisted to my kids they needed to watch it with their dad. I saw *No Mercy* which me had crying for the entire day. I just kept thinking that today we were worse off as a country then we were when *Roots* took place. I thought to myself I would rather be a slave and get raped (as they did prior to the civil war) then be in jail on death row for a crime I didn't commit. At least Kunta Kinte had a wife who loved him and kids who loved him at the end of each day. Kunta Kinte also got to live. These men were being killed on death row, today in our country. I hated the characters in the movie, the bad cops, the bad lawyers, and the bad judges. *Racist mother fuckers*, I thought. I watched Richard Jewel and my heart was broken once again. How in the world did we get here as a country? Richard was the sweetest. He was on the spectrum, and he was good. He was kind. He was a hero. The FBI, ugh! Liars, ego maniacs, lazy! Every institution in America is broken, It's all broken. I cried more that week in the Arlo Hotel than I have ever cried in my life. Each night after about two hours of sleep, I would wake up around 1 am and walk aimlessly around Soho for hours. I would cry and cry and cry. I would pick up all the trash on the ground and put it in the garbage. It was NYC and picking up the trash was keeping me very busy at night. I seriously thought I had to die to save my children. I didn't want to die but I wanted to save my children.

My hotel bill was getting fat and I was almost out of one hundred-dollar bills. I went shopping for my kids at Target in Soho. I spent $1200 on outfits for the party that I thought was happening at the Arlo Hotel. I was telling the people at the front desk my boys were coming to see me from Chicago. In my mind, I was planning to go to a huge party with Kobe Bryant and Vanessa. I thought Kobe was alive. I face-timed my kids about the party and they were laughing at me. They were also very concerned. Day after day my kids didn't show up and the party wasn't happening. My kids kept telling me to go home and so I finally after a five-night-and-six-day stay, I went back to my apartment.

Once I was back to my apartment things for me seemed to get even worse. I still couldn't sleep, hardly a wink since March 2nd. I would find myself walking aimlessly in Central Park in the middle of the night. Cops would be on their speaker at 3:00 am, "The Park is now closed; please exit the park." I thought I would die and then my book, *A true Unicorn* would be published, and my kids would see to it that *NOoodle* was a big success. It was my birthday that would become a movement to save our country and our world, "March 4th in love." I just didn't want to die. I thought for the movement, "March 4th in love" to be successful, it needed me, an empath leader to lead the way. I didn't want to die, I wanted to live. I wanted to fight for justice and equality. Alex and Jake and the millions of kids of the Gen Amazing generation were going to march to Washington and remove Donald Trump from office. They were going to take the President's seat and full power and they were going to change all the inequalities that exist in our country today.

I clearly had lost my mind. The thing about losing your mind that I learned from losing my mind is that when you are lost in your mind you don't realize it. Everything you're thinking and experiencing is real. The tears are real, the sadness is real, the anxiety is real. The mind has taken over the physical body.

Looking back, I remember it was day two at the Arlo Hotel in Soho when I declared to myself, "I am a vegetarian!" I said out loud. During my stay I had one of the most amazing cheeseburgers and then the next day I had the most amazing chicken wings and French fries, three of my favorite foods. I don't throw away food and Arlo had a mini fridge in my room. The following day I started to eat the cold burger and the cold chicken wings. It was during this experience that my brain completely got so grossed out by the idea of eating meat I threw it all away. The skin on the wings, it was suddenly disgusting to me, and I have been eating Buffalo Chicken wings almost my entire life. I vowed to myself I would never eat meat again. At least that is what my thoughts were telling me at that moment. I was sure of it; I was vegetarian from now on. I also taught myself the correct way to recycle. All the meals were brought in to go containers. The Arlo was known for being a recyclable friendly hotel, totally cool, totally hip for business travelers and I loved it. I stayed there last year when *NOoodle* was exhibiting at the Fancy food Show at the Javits center. Now the Javits was a hospital for Covid patients.

When I got back to my apartment, my LinkedIn page was gone, never to return. My *NOoodle* Facebook with over 11,000 followers wiped out. My own personal Facebook with over 4000 friends, gone. My website, *NOoodle*, was offline. I did notice I had some unread emails. I scrolled them quickly and found this one from my contact at Super

Frec Foods, USA. The factory which makes my product line also 100% of my supply chain.

On March 26th, 2020, at 5:30 pm:

Hi Terri,

I hope this email finds you well.

We wanted to let you know that due to this whole COVID-19 coronavirus situation, we do not have any space for orders for April and May. We hope for your understanding during these difficult times.

Best Regards,
Nelson Matsuda
Client Relationship Manager
Super Frec USA

I remember my head spinning out of control. My brain and my company were hacked. How did they do it to my brain? I know…they hacked my brain during the five eye surgeries I had. I thought my eyes were cameras recording everyone and everything I encountered.

I heard months later that people were calling my kids. Several of my friends and business associates thought I died in NYC during Covid. The crazy thing is most of my closest family members and closest friends never called me. Candy, my sister, my mother, my father, they never called. I assumed they didn't want anything to do with me after I ended up in the hospital on my birthday. I guess that happens when someone goes temporarily insane during a pandemic. At least that is what I believed in the moment which made me even worse! I felt so alone in the world and so scared.

During the next couple of days, I remember walking around the UWS and giving away all my things to the homeless. I gave away my fur coat, I gave away my diamond necklace. I gave away more hundred-dollar bills. I was so sad for the homeless. I would fall asleep during the day and wake up fifteen minutes later feeling as if I slept for hours. I would wake up every night from terrible dreams. Sometimes I would wake up from songs and then I would sing them for the entire night and the next day.

One of the songs happens to be by REM, "If you believe…we put a man on the moon, man on the moon. If you believe there is nothing up our sleeve and nothing is good." I think I sang those lyrics to over fifty people one day. I had created my own conspiracy theory in my mind about why the coronavirus was happening. My conspiracy theory is extremely positive. I was always positive – always seeing the glass half full.

A few days later, I ended up taking a taxi to O'Hare and buying a one-way ticket to Chicago. The next flight to Chicago was eight hours later so I waited. I met a woman from Huntsville, Alabama, a nurse who flew in to help the first responders in NYC. She told me of her experience. She said never in her life has she seen so much death. She said these men were healthy in their thirties, forties, fifties. It was surreal for her and all she wanted to do was go home to her husband and dogs. She would share some of her experiences and then she would go back to the book she was reading. I asked her what her book was about. She said it was a book during WW2 on how the Nazis were doing experiments on Human beings. She said the book she was reading was fiction. *Interesting*, I thought.

I had recently seen the show, *Hunters* on Amazon Prime, starring Al Pacino. Did you know that the USA government hand-picked 2200 of the most skilled doctors and scientists from Nazi Germany after the War and brought them to our country and set them up with new names and jobs? It's called 'Operation paperclips.' Many of them went to work and many of these Nazi's were living in Huntsville, Alabama. Maybe that is why my brain told me to start singing REM's song. Maybe REM was right. Maybe we never did go to the moon after all. Maybe instead there was something up our government's sleeves that was good?

My kids weren't expecting me. I had no phone, and I didn't bring my computer. It crashed from my POV. I couldn't do anything, so I didn't need it. Not to mention I was out of business for the next 60 to 90 days since my supply was shut off.

Last night, I Facetimed Jake and Alex from my mac. I was crying and saying goodbye to them as if I was going to die in my sleep. They ended up calling the cops who came to my apartment. I pretended I was not there and didn't answer my door. I didn't want to go to the hospital. I thought I would die of covid if I did.

On the plane I passed out. When I woke up, we were getting ready for landing. My ears were ringing, and my mind was telling me that I was crazy. How am I supposed to explain to my kids that I thought we were going to a party with Vanessa and Kobe? I realized I would tell them what I really was trying to say. Kobe is alive in all of us, that is

43

what I meant. He is alive in our hearts and lives on thru us. Okay but that is *not* what I believed a few days ago.

I finally arrived in Buffalo Grove, Illinois. I lugged all the clothing I had just bought for the parties (that were a figment of my imagination). I even bought a gift for my ex-husband. They wouldn't let me in. I had just come from the epicenter of Death, NYC, and I could infect them with the virus. I dropped all the bags of things I bought for them, and I started walking away, my heart was broken. I was sad and mad. I was crying. I was also physically exhausted. I started walking to Deerfield. My son drives up with his mask on and insists on me getting in the car which I did. He said he would take me to a hotel, but he would rather check me into a hospital. I told him to drive me to my longtime friend Scott's house. Jake didn't think he would let me in, but he did.

I woke up the next morning as I usually did about two hours after I fell asleep, this time it was 2:30 am. I ended up leaving my friend Scott's house and walked to the town of Highland Park, Il. where I had my second restaurant location. I walked around the covid ghost town until the sun came up. I stopped in a coffee shop I knew, she let me use the phone to call a taxi to take me back to O'Hare. At the terminal, the only flight I could get was the following morning. I spent the night at the Hilton in the terminal. It was the coolest experience; I got a corner suite that overlooked many tarmacs. Normally you would be able to watch many, many planes land from my room but not on this night. No planes were taking off. I didn't notice any that landed either I thought to myself, *wow!* What a great way to save the planet and correct our air. This pandemic is starting to look like a gift from God. Well God made it anyway since mother nature is responsible for creating this virus. She has spoken again, "Ground the planes. Remove the need for macro-movement globally. Introduce the need to produce and buy locally," she said to me in my head. *Wow…mother nature, i.e., God, they really are wickedly smart*, I thought.

I arrived back at my apartment completely exhausted. I slept on the plane. I also went through my experiences in the month of march and calculated the hours that I slept in the month of March. I averaged about two hours each night. I included the 15-minute cat naps during the day. I realized no one wants to kill me. I realized no one is going to be marching to DC to remove the president. I started Googling what happens when we go a month without sleeping. There were many articles that were telling me this can create mental illness. *I had to really try to get rest*, I thought.

The next day I get a text from Jake he writes, "*U have the power. Look up Selena Gomez-bipolar revelation. It is scary to face but once faced we can conquer it.*"

I write, "*Thank you, Jake. I know I have the power. Tom gave me words of wisdom this morning. I have had the worst thirty-five days of my life. I can only try and focus on what I can do today to add value into the world. I am going to start cooking and donating my time for the first responders at the hospital. I hope it helps keep my mind off my troubles. I am so sorry to have burdened you. Love you, Mom.*"

Jake writes, "*Who is Tom?*"

I write, "*Tom Train Coco's husband. I think I have a good case of the self-fulfilling prophecy. My entire family thinks I am crazy so therefore I am. I am going to focus on getting better my way and not the way of my family, i.e.,* taking prescription drugs. I really don't want anything to do with my family anymore. They have not been there for me for a long time, and I don't need to be brought down by trying to get approval and love from them. Please do not speak my name to them anymore as actions speak louder than words. They all have proved through their actions that they would allow me to be insane and homeless than do something to help me. I never needed their help, and I don't need their help now either. Mom."

Jake writes, "That's messed up. You would be making decisions on bs.. Get healthy, Mom! You're not okay. So prideful that it can't be done any other way? Weird. Love you, Mom. Have a good day."

I write, "Okay...weird, whatever. I am just in a hurt position right now. I can't explain to you what I am going through because you wouldn't understand. I am having huge bi-polar swings. I am hopeful this too shall pass."

Jake writes, "It will pass by actions. Getting help. Ur in a hard position, we see that clearly. Writing about your family is weird. You need to get help and we are here to aid u in getting that help."

I write, "I am getting help by offering my time to the first responders of the coronavirus. I need to get out of my head, and I don't want to go on any medication. I am sorry if it's not your way or my sister or my mother's way. I need to do this my way first."

Jake writes, "My way isn't medication. It's getting a specialist and talking to them. Realizing why ur hurting, realizing what steps u can do to ease the hurting."

I write, "I am not writing them off, but it is interesting that not one of them contacted me during this time specifically since I am alone in NYC. It's just disappointing. If I didn't expect anything, I would not be disappointed."

Jake writes, "*If the dr. says hey if u do 20 push-ups a day, it will get rid of ur attacks. Wud u do 20 push-ups a day? Of course! It's just about getting info and having a conversation about ur health. Mom u haven't had a phone for several weeks maybe longer. We can only text message u when ur on your computer. When ur not using your computer, my texts don't go thru.*"

I write, "*I know why I am hurting...my business was doing great and now it's in a dead stand still. I am not in control of it and the only thing I can do right now is except that I am not in control and focus my efforts on something I can control like working and helping the first responders. I need to start connecting again with others which is the greatest thing missing today which is causing me unwanted pain.*"

Jake writes, "*Okay, I like those steps. Taking action. Why not call a therapist? Literally a dr. that just listens. Anyway, I am sorry about ur business it's messed up.*"

A day has passed, and I am writing to Jake again. "*Hi Jake...thank you for telling me to watch the movie, Frozen. I am almost done with the first movie. I am a bit like Princess Elsa...desperate for love. I don't want to alienate myself from my family. I love them very much as you know. I am going to start taking a deeper look into myself to realize that my life and all its sadness and all its glory has been created by my own design and demise. In fact, If I allow myself to implode, which I will not. I have been good at being attached to outcomes and blaming others for my mistakes and misfortunes. I have learned mostly because of not being patient with the process. I am lucky to have been able to have you and your brother. I remember the biggest compliment grandma has given me in a long time, in forever. She told me recently that the reason why you and your brother are so loving is because I am so loving. Thank you for being my son. I am incredibly proud and humbled. I am sorry that I have been weak and have made poor choices when it comes to love. I know I don't need to be sorry about that to you and your brother, but I need to truly forgive myself if I am ever to become the great loving human being. Not only to my family, to you and Alex, to all strangers but also to myself. Most importantly, I need to love myself. I need to honor my word as myself and my word is love."*

Jake writes, *"Watch Frozen two too."*

I write, *"Thank you. I will keep watching the movie now. I won't be dying of a broken heart anytime soon. It is my heart that is my biggest strength and I have faith today. Now that I will be able to use it fully not only to help others but also one day when the time is right, romantic love will find me. One day I will have that love again too. Please share this with your brother."*

Jake writes, *"I did. (-: Love you too."*

Another day passes.

I write to Jake, *"Thank you. I am very blessed. I am going to focus on what I can control over the next coming days. I guess Aunt Lulu is right about one thing when she suggested, 'A great life is not about passion, a great life is about adding value.' A great life is simply about adding value where and when we can and specifically helping others. I forgot or was mistaken about my idea regarding 'the power of being poor.' The true value in being poor is we still can help others, strangers, loved ones, all of us. I guess I forget who I was, and my ego took over. It seems as if I was out to prove something to all the naysayers specifically my family. When all they wanted me to do was realize that I wasn't NOoodle. I was just me. Terri. Just…I say just but it is not just, it is so much, so big. I am a woman who is fortunate to be a mom. Fortunate to be a daughter of a great mom and a great stepmom. A woman who is a daughter to a great dad and stepdad. A woman who is fortunate to have a great beautiful sister and a great loving brother. A woman who is fortunate to have two half-brothers and one-half sister. A woman who is fortunate to have my brother-in-law and two amazing sisters-in-law. A woman who has four nephews and four nieces. I think I am going to give up NOoodle and do something else. It has not really brought me much happiness. In the end, the only thing that matters is happiness and love."*

Jake writes, *"Okay. Very nice. If you want to give up NOoodle, I'd like you to give up on it by passing it off to me and or Alex. We can take over and continue the possibility u created. NOoodle isn't of the utmost importance right now. Can talk about it later. Keep up the positivity, and plz get some sleep tonight."*

I write, *"NOoodle has brought me much sadness and loneliness. I think it is because I was trying to prove something instead of just doing what I love to do which is cook for people and love people and that is really what brings me the most joy. I think the most important thing I can do right now today is of service to others. The best way I know how right now is to help the first responders by cooking and feeding them. It is my true joy to cook for those I love. I always say love is right here in our hearts so whoever is in front of us is the person/people who we get to love. I wish I can change my passcode to my computer. It is A True Unicorn. That is not really who I am today. Who I am today is a true love?*

"*I believe today a true love is someone who loves all people good. I believe what I am so desperately missing is a community here in NYC. I am going to work harder to attain it. I have some money saved and they won't evict me here for three months so I can use that time to help the less fortunate. Passion is overrated but hard work overtime thru loving others is where it is at! I am truly sorry I put you and your brother thru this. I will get better. You are right, today is only one day. Today is going to be a good day and tomorrow will be a good day and then Monday should be a great day because I started my new job I created. In a way, I have only just begun. I will cook for all those amazing people who are helping to save so many lives. I will cook for those who don't have a home. It's hard to believe that I didn't see this clearly until now. I guess sometimes the most obvious of things are the hardest to see. I love you, kid! Mom.*"

The next day I wake up to a text from Jake, he writes, "*Love you too. I will also have your back.*"

I write, "*You always have my back. I have just been a bit selfish these days. I thought I was selfless but that was a big lie I was telling myself. I have been selfish. I am going to change that through my actions over.*

Jake writes *Also, Uncle Simon says it might be that you have an outstanding balance with GoDaddy, he thinks that is why your website is down.*"

I write, "*No outstanding balance with GoDaddy.*"

Another day passes. I write, "*Jake…I am switching cell phone providers, so you need to do the following if you want me to pay for your cell phone number. First you need to call spectrum to route your new service. They will ask for your Apple information.*"

I had a chance to reflect on the text Tom Train wrote to me that got myself in action. He wrote, "*Terri, organize in your building your neighbors to donate funds. Go to a restaurant or a pizza place which does take out. Place a large order with them and take the pizzas to the emergency room of a hospital. Talk to a restaurant to help with cooking and takeout meals. You are a resourceful lady and make it happen for other people. The interaction with the right people and your neighbors will reduce your loneliness and your urge to look at the garbage on the internet. I am paying six guys in my business to stay employed and busy, even though we had a lot of cancellations. You can apply for government assistance because you're a small business. All these things could keep you active and from thinking negative thoughts. No, you're not a robot. Remember I always called you iron-woman because you're a very strong person, Terri. Good luck and stay busy. Tom Sr.*"

As soon as I received his text, I wrote him back. I wrote, "*Thanks, Tom…I will start working on this right now. Love you. I feel as if I am losing my mind. I will concentrate on helping others. Maybe this will be what I need to help my mind calm down.*"

Today I wrote Tom the following, *"Tom...I can't explain to you how much your note has helped me in a short period of time. You showed me what I couldn't see. I was struggling here beyond words. I was so afraid that all I was thinking about was myself. I can't believe how awful I was being. Prior to covid, I said terrible things to my family. I told them all that if NOoodle didn't work I would rather die. I know today that I don't want to die. Regardless of the success or failure of NOoodle. I wanted to get back, get even, on everyone in business who lied to me along the way. I wanted to blame others so that I could be right. I couldn't even see the forest through the trees. All I wanted to do was blame everyone for not helping me when it wasn't anyone's responsibility to help me in the first place. You are right, I am the iron lady. I am supposed to help others, not the other way around. I lay here wondering where I went wrong...again. I know it is my ego. It is always my ego. Not only that but my ego was lying to me. I pretended it was everyone else's fault, everyone else's ego. After you texted me last week, I got in touch with the head guy at my local Mt. Sinai urgent care. I will be helping the first responders by cooking them vegetarian meals. I can make great rice and potato meals which are inexpensive to make so I can feed many. I am so grateful to you and Coco for your love and friendship. If all I had in the world were the Train family, I would be a very lucky woman. I have so much more love than that. It is hard to see our true selves. We tack on a lot of layers of smoke and mirrors at times. I have a very small kitchen. I can cook a lot of food if I am organized. People are dying and no one deserves to die, and yet we all do. I am so happy that you have Coco, and she has you. One* day I know I will find that love. Thank you for inspiring my life in a great big way. Love, Terri."

Tom writes, "*Wow, Terri! I am amazed by all the words you put down here. This is you! If I was able to put you in the right frame of mind with just a few words, it seems as if you found your true self again. Coco and I are so happy and proud of you. Through helping people by cooking for them, offering them unconditional support, you will not have to look for the right man. He will show himself to you when the time is right. Just make sure you stay safe, wear gloves, and use masks. You are in a warzone there. Consider all the doctors, nurses, medical assistants who are in bigger danger than you are. Through your personal sacrifice, helping them, you will find lots of new friends. You will not be alone there anymore. Doing these selfless actions, you will find that your family and your kids will be very proud. Just stay safe, stay strong. This will be over soon. When you feel that you're getting a bit down and depressed, read up on the short introduction and watch the videos of my book I sent you. Most Americans don't know what it is to make the sacrifices, to lose yourself and find yourself in this vast world, building a family from nothing. I am not scared of what is going on here in the USA. Not yet. In comparing all this with what I already have gone through, this is just a correction for the people of this world. I think this may be a great chance and a serious lesson for the American people and for the people of the world at large. As people were all in the same boat and to solve this problem we need to work together. Only love can conquer anything God is watching. Help yourself and help others and God will be with you. If you need some funds, we could wire you some. Let us know where. You can also apply to SBA for a loan at your bank because you have a business. They can tell you how. Coco and I love you and are very proud of you. Keep us informed. Tom Sr."*

I wrote, *"Thank you, Tom, for being a dear friend. I love you both too."*

Another day passes, each day seems to last forever. I write to my son Alex. *"Alex...I am completely shut out of my entire company. I believe I have been hacked. Now I can't get access to any of my money."*

Alex writes, *"Mom, I am sorry I just accidentally said I didn't do a transaction for $55 to spectrum. I don't know why it was sent to my phone number. But now it says your card ending in 4095 is locked and they are sending you a new one to your address. I am so sorry. This is all so confusing. How can I help? We are here to help?"*

I write, *"It is okay, Alex. I told you I have been hacked. Not only my computer but also my brain. I have not been able to sleep more than an hour or two since March 1st. My head is in great pain, and I know I need to sleep. For some reason I am afraid to close my eyes."*

Alex writes, *"Goodnight. Love you, call you tomorrow."*

I wrote to him, *"I know me too. I know what I told you and your brother. I know no one believes me but what if what I was saying is true. What if I was the princess in Frozen riding the unicorn to save the world? I only wish you and Jake believed me. I was never crazy, just crazy for you and your brother. I wish you could just talk to me until I fall asleep tonight. It hurts my whole body is in physical pain."*

Alex writes, "*I have homework. It's fine. Drink water. Eat food. Relax. Listen to music. Take a nap.*"

I write, "*Okay, Aunt Daisy says tomorrow I have the Zoom call with Dr. I know it is hard to believe but you guys will be billionaires and our world will be saved. Daisy says I would have sleep apnea and maybe die in my sleep, but I don't have sleep apnea, this is not that. This is different. Watch 1917. The Irish officer Blaire at the end is the spitting image of you. I believe he was my Irish grandfather. My mom said her dad was very handsome and mean and died before I was born. What if it was true that he was a big officer and part of the future to save the world? Is it not possible if you believe? Why can't we imagine the impossible? Why can't we believe that there is a bigger, more powerful idea? Victor Hugo said, 'There is nothing more powerful than an idea whose time has come.' In the future, social media will no longer be. Eating meat will be outlawed along with cigarettes and all drugs except cannabis. Remember who I am, my ears continue to ring, and they hurt.*

The next day I heard back from Daisy. She wrote, "*Terri I confirmed your appointment. Call me it's in ten minutes. Pick up your phone.*"

I wrote, "*Hi Daisy...I am on my way to give out NOoodle meals with City meals. I do believe what I told you to be true. Either way I don't want to get on drugs as I believe drugs are not healthy. I understand that you and Simon are on these drugs, but I have never been on these types of drugs. I don't want to start now. I want to focus my efforts on helping and hopefully I will get myself back to normal. The first thing I need to do is start sleeping more* than an hour a night. You did me a very big favor by helping get my business and emails back on track. I think that was a big reason I was feeling so alone and confused."

She writes, "*Terri, you are going to end up with many problems if you don't get help.*"

I wrote, "*Daisy...you have already helped me tremendously by getting my company and website back online. It was hacked and I have been very paranoid of the last few weeks because of it. I can't take any meds that are manufactured. It goes against my being. I also believe what I told you to be true. I know it sounds crazy but maybe it could be true. You said you watched the movie 1917 and the years don't make sense. Blaire was about 23 years old in the movies which means he was born around 1897 which would have made him exactly 50 years old when my mom was born in 1947. My mom told me he was an older father.*

Anyway, I see how you and Simon are with your kids and it seems like the meds you guys are on are not really helping either one of you cope. The way Simon talked to Pheona yesterday while I was on the phone from my POV was extremely crazy too. I guess we all are a little crazy. I do thank you for helping me get my company, NOoodle, back online. It was freaking me out. You were my only adult family member that took the time out of your day to help me. We were friends before we were family. Love you, Daisy."

Daisy writes, "*Cool, where is the music party in NYC?*"

I write, "*Yes...I thought it was everywhere at 7:00 pm but it is just in NYC. Maybe it is just on my block I am not sure. At 7:00 pm everyone stands outside and plays loud on their drums or claps or yells. It is kind of cool. Are they doing this in Boca? It is a way for everyone to say hi to each other from their stoop and or the front of their buildings. It lasts for three minutes and then everyone goes back inside. How are you doing today? I hope the kids are treating you with respect. You really love those kids, and you deserve for them to respect you. I know it is hard raising teenagers and you have the best positive attitude always. It is my favorite thing about you...your positivity. Tomorrow night I will FaceTime you at 7:00 pm so you can experience it with me, virtually.*

I send a text to my son Alex, "*Are you getting my texts?*"

He writes, "*I am not communicating with you until you get on medication. I am sorry. You are in denial. You need anti-psychotic medication. It is not a bad thing mom it's just what you need.*"

I wrote back, "*That is your choice, sometimes things are not always what they seem. Just forget what I said. I was struggling with isolation anxiety combined with my company being hacked. I am trying to get everything back online. I am feeling a little better now that I have access to my work emails. Hopefully soon I will be able to resolve my banking information. I believe I am back on track and will not have any more psychotic episodes. I do not want to take meds because I am against everything they stand for. I started cooking vegetarian meals and I am giving them away to the homeless in Central Park. Also please send this link (The 5 worst foods for Arthritis) to your nana. I believe she may not be up today on the foods you shouldn't eat if you suffer from arthritis.*"

I reached out to my 71-year-old friend Jan. His name is pronounced Yan, but it is spelled with a J. I guess that is how they do things in South Africa which is where good old' Jan is from.

I texted, "*Hi Jan...I heard that you were talking about me 'going crazy' to my family. Instead of calling me back and being my friend, you went behind my back and gossiped about me to my family who all they do is gossip about others, from my POV. You were always two-faced. Everyone who knows you says it. Dee said it to me. She told me that you were always saying mean things to her about me. Claudia told me you were always saying mean things to her about me and now I know that you continue to be a two-faced person. Perhaps that is the reason why I was your only true friend, WAS is the key word. I will always love you and you have great potential but until you see the ugly in' you your life will continue to be what it is. Going nowhere but to meditation, aka the light. To me the light in this regard is death. Yup I said it. Not death as death but death because meditation is a very alone and lonely space. I believe it should be practiced 5-20 minutes a day to clear our minds out. Mindful-less-ness is essential to a powerful mind. 'Everything is moderation' is a great saying for a reason, it's true. You seem to practice it all day long every day and that is just weird! Yes, I said it...weird and lonely and alone.*

I did have some major sadness in March but instead of dwelling on the sadness. I decided to do something about it now. I am cooking vegetarian meals and giving them away in the park. I have also given away $3000, in one-hundred-dollar bills to the homeless here. I just gave my diamond necklace to this sweet and beautiful homeless woman. I didn't think she was homeless. She looked amazing.

Anyway, I have given away most of my clothes to the homeless too. How much money have you donated? I guess all that meditation has brought you NO WHERE NEAR THE LIGHT from my POV. Now that you are so chum-chum-chummy with the Fanast Family why don't you share this text with them and ask them how much money they have donated to the first responders? Donated to people who are without a home, without food, without anything. I bet the answer is ZERO. Who is crazy now?"

Jan responded with, *"Please cease and desist from communicating with me. By the way I said nothing negative about you to anyone ever. I told Mike that you decided to stay in NYC and be of help. By the way is Kobe alive? If there is truth to be told I have always been fair and compassionate. Claudia and Dee said un-redeeming negative things about you, and I always defended with reasonable understanding. After all negativity that stick is a chance for missed understanding. And as for what contribution I have made. I had major surgery on the 10th of March and have been unable to walk. So, make your own contribution and keep your ego out of the comparisons currently. Please refrain from contacting me. I saw James the manager at the lemon tree at Home Depot yesterday where he now works. They shuttered all restaurants and fired everyone without pay or past bills owed so before you give away another $1000 send me $400. Po. box 3404, Sarasota, Fl 34230."*

I write, *"Jan...thank you for all the information. Kobe is alive and well right here in ALL our hearts. That is what I was intending to mean. The social distancing and isolation have taken a toll on everyone, and I did suffer some degree* *of depression but thankfully I am out of the woods and on to new and better things like helping our world become a cleaner, healthier, and more loving environment. As for the $400 you think I owe you...start taking responsibility for your choices and actions. You're a 70-year-old baby. I still love you and Dee and Claudia. We ALL are two faced to some degree. We ALL talk bad about the people we love and the people that we don't love. I guess it is called being human. Unfortunately, by making other people wrong we think it in turn makes us right. It doesn't, it just makes us two faced and gossipers. Right off the $400, add it to the grossly large sum of money that you decided to put into the slot machines. What a VERY STUPID WAY to spend your money. You should have just thrown it away in the garbage. Good luck, Jan...I truly wish you the best in all your future endeavors."*

Jan writes, *"That $400 request was a joke! Seems like you lost your great sense of humor momentarily. And your sanctimonious comment re my choices was unwelcome maternalistic and might be reserved for your children."*

I write, *"Sounds good, Jan. I have no hard feelings. I love you and want your life to be great. My company is now on a better track. Perhaps in the future I will have a job for you. I will let you know when that happens."*

Jan sends me a picture of a lion and writes, *"Me since arriving back in SRQ since you accuse me of being two faced!"*

I write, *"Listen we are all two-faced. I am a lion too. You are my dear friend and I love you! When this is over you need to come back to NYC where you belong. I need you next to me with NOoodle. You are Arjuna, remember?*

Also, I am talking to HUGH, he is awesome. What a nice man and I am going to make him one of my company's advisors one day. I really would like you to come back to NYC and work for GENamaZing, we are going to do amazing things with lime from Ethiopia and silver infused in foods. There is so much information out there and people are just so ignorant, and it is time for a big change. We need to illuminate the world from sickness from the current foods we eat. I have been eating about 6 tablespoons of Ikura a day. In addition to eggs and cheese this is where I am sourcing most of the protein I am ingesting today."

I received another message from Daisy, my friend first now my sister-in-law, regarding the empathy support line. I write, *"Hi, Daisy…I told you I am not interested but I really thank you for your concern. I do believe I had some upset and some psychopathic symptoms. I am trying to put it in my past. I am doing great things to add value into the world today. I would suggest you and Simon both take Chris Voss masterclass. I am starting it today. Love you for caring. Your friend and sister Terri. Ps…get off the meds. I am sure if you are honest with yourself, you are not feeling good or looking your best. It is because you are not digesting healthy foods and you are on meds that are designed to slowly kill you. Party is on in two minutes."*

I wrote a text to my friend Julia who just lost her mom. We met on the chair lift on Breckenridge Mountain. She had asked me what I was doing today. My response. *"Hi, Julia. We are going to be in Central Park giving NOoodle meals and doing protocol fitness. It is great today here in NYC because they can take New York but they can't take the New Yorker out of New York. Soon you must come for a visit,* girl! Are you still practicing our 90-day rule? The good thing for me is that I have not had any desire for any man so keeping our 90-day rule has been quite an easy task. We must continue to move our idea forward in a big and great way! The 90-day rule is a new rule in our world that will set us all free of getting involved in the wrong relationship. 90dayrule; only kissing, holding hands, and cuddling when others are in the room. See you soon in NYC girly. So glad we met on the slopes of Breckenridge, Colorado."

Text was the only way I could communicate since I still had no phone, and we are sheltering in place. My friend, Abbe, lives on the other side of Central Park, I reached out with a text. "Hi, sweetie...it is going to be a great day! I made some food, and I am going to take a stake in the park and give away premade NOoodle meals and bags of NOoodle. If you want, you can meet Chris and me. We are self-distancing and doing protocol. I will let you know the time. Love you, keep up your positive attitude...soon this too shall pass."

Abbe writes, "Good morning. I'm staying inside this week. But thx. Please be careful and watch ur allergies. U don't want to go to the hospital now. I watched through my window someone collapse on the sidewalk yesterday. I'm staying positive but it sucks my friend lost his dad yesterday, client died, my parents' childhood friend died. It's horrible right now. I am good tho."

I write back, "Abbe-Scott's phone is not registered because I am still waiting for a SIM card. I cannot text him. Please forward this message to him for me please. Thank you, xoxoxo.

"Hi Scott...it's Terri. I am sorry I left that day and left all those notes to you regarding recycling and being a vegetarian and nationalizing our food sources. As you know I didn't come to visit you. I came to Chicago last week to visit my kids. The way they rejected me along with the fact that I was under a lot of stress I just didn't want to be there. You were so sweet to let me in as you always are a great friend. I know that you didn't want me in your house since I just left covid NYC. I knew you were paranoid about me being there and getting you sick, so I left. I am extremely confident one day all meat will be banned along with the fact that we will; have all our food products made in the USA. This is the future I am living into as one of the leaders of the future of food. I love you so much, Scott. One day my story of perseverance will be heard in all its great glory. Big business is starting to give back and I believe this is just the beginning of the great progress for humanity that has come from this great breakdown. Today I am going to do protocol in the park and give out NOoodle meals and NOoodle like we used to. It is beautiful here and the death toll is finally starting to subside. It is a new day...love you! Terri."

Chapter 4

"Industry, Lose No Time. Always Be Employed with Something Useful." – Ben Franklin

April 8th: Shakipat initiation, the awakening of Kundalini Shakti is the supreme act of the master's grace. It is the lightning bolt that reveals the greatest treasure within. It is the ultimate gesture of compassion, the breath of the Absolute that breaks the chains of endless death and rebirth and sets you free once and for all.

When Kundalini Shakti is awakened by the master's grace, the knot of the heart is released. All Karmas, all sins, are being washed away and the pure Being is revealed within. That Being is the embodiment of wisdom, light, and truth. Gurumayi Chidvilasananda

I recently learned back in the day all the president's men were sworn in and out on one day, March 4th. I was born on March 4th 1969. My birthday spells out what we need to do as a country to get through this awful morass we find our country in today. March 4th in love. We must do this together today and every day. All the moms together led by mother nature herself. We are the real life 'Mother of dragons and breaker of chains.'

April 9th, 2020, 7:58 am I text, "*Good morning, Jake. I signed you up for a Master Class subscription. You are going to love it! It is so educational and perfect for you right now. Please check it out today when you have some time. You should start running outside every day. I am the first to tell you how it feels to have a mental break due to the stress of what's happening in our world today. I wasn't working out and I think the anxiety of this event and not being with any family and not working out took me to a place where I never want to be again. We must work out our bodies every day and eat healthy. It is our number one job as human beings today to ourselves. Love you, Mom.*"

I sent Jake and Alex a picture that had the caption: *Chynna Rogers was a drug addict plagued by demons that haunted her till the tragic end.*

I wrote, "*I hope you guys NEVER take hard drugs again. Drugs kill and cannabis should be used in moderation. One thing that happened to me through my covid breakdown is I became more passionate about all living things as a part of GOD. I know they were part of GOD, but I was eating them anyway. Chicken, cow, turkey, frogs, pigs, I was eating all animals. I have been a vegetarian now for several weeks and for me this is the only way our people and our planet will be able to 'March 4th in love.' We need to start protecting mother nature's creations. I feel strong in my resolve to help our planet and eco system. The good news is I still get to eat the biproducts of animals, i.e., cheese, eggs, dairy. I had a big mac the other day. I ordered it without meat, extra lettuce, extra pickles. I didn't miss the meat patties at all. I still have not tried any of the meat like protein, i.e., beyond meat. I also*

65

know that we have been importing most everything we consume in our bodies and that is hurting our environment. Also, we are eating veggies and fruits that are genetically modified. I believe humans have created all the diseases and reasons we die young. Diabetes, Cancer, heart disease, celiac disease, dairy intolerances, anaphylaxis, arthritis, and now covid-19. Here is a link that explains what I was suffering from. Everyone is different and anxiety takes on all forms, I guess. I attached an article with the saying, 'isolation is a big trigger, negative thinking is amplified amid a pandemic.'"

Today is April 12th, 2020, Easter. The world has come to know NYC as the epicenter of coronavirus. Most of the people I know who had second homes were running scared out of the city by mid-March, they vacated immediately. NYC felt like a ghost town. Isolated and confused many of us, including myself, suffered alone. My friends and family are still gone from NYC, I wonder if they will ever come back?

NYC is the epicenter of love. People from all walks of life, a beautiful example of the United Nations all working together in one little, tiny island. We have a bull as our President. We have Joe Biden as his number one opponent. We have social distancing in place. A city and a country divided by elected officials who (from my POV) are more interested in being 'right' instead of being effective.

My situation today is a situation that has arisen out of my duty to help the masses of people who are suffering. We have a huge choice to make as American citizens. Do we want to live into a future that resembles our past? Not I, said the fly. Not me, said the bee.

Everyone knows mother nature is the biggest serial killer. I have faith that everything in our lives happens for the greater good. Did you know that over twenty countries have nuclear capabilities who wanted to see America explode? We were correct if we feared a nuclear exchange. We still are correct when we fear a nuclear exchange. An exchange for those of you who don't know, it would be a slow death for all humanity worldwide. This is a 'scientific observational truth'.

Climate change aka, as REM sings, "It's the end of the world as we know it. It's the end of the world as we know it." Another scientific observational truth, google the thousands of scientists who have proof to back it up. We have a president who has completely dropped the ball. Now…if I told you because I am a leader in the future of food that in the year 2080, on the course we are going on, we will *not* be able to grow any more food. 2080 is our *last* year of harvest. If we don't die of a nuclear exchange, we will die of starvation in the year 2080. Don't take my word for it, please google it. You will learn that this is another 'scientific observational truth.' I told my stepmom this a few weeks ago and she replied, "Why do you care, you will be dead by then." Well, do you want my short answer or my long answer? I didn't give her either because a stupid question doesn't warrant a response. As Forest Gump says, "Stupid is as stupid does." Here is my long answer: In 2080, I will still be alive and kicking, hopefully skiing double black diamonds, who knows? It is not for me that I care so much today. It is for Alex and Jake and all the other children in our world. Their lives will be cut short at 83 and 81 years young. It is for their children, our grandchildren, and their grandchildren. I believe my stepmom has a different kind of brain. A brain that is not a mother or a father. My short answer is I care because I am a mother. I am a mother of dragons (to Jake and Alex). Today I believe it is my duty to not only be "the mother of dragons *but also* the breaker of chains." I believe it is my duty, our duty, to save our world from complete annihilation. As a leader of the future of food. As a mother, a chef, a friend, a daughter, a sister, a teacher, a student, a philomath, a skier, a singer, and a lover of all people who are good; I am going to fight to repair our planet so heaven on earth will continue indefinitely.

Did you know a huge part of our workforce here in America are underpaid and underappreciated? We are not playing fair. The game, the rules, need to be reworked and redefined. Many companies are not paying taxes. Many companies are cheating their employees. We now know, thanks to coronavirus, over 90% of our workforce is non-essential. It means 90% of our workforce are going to need new jobs, jobs that are essential to life. Donald Trump wants to re-open the economy? The rich continue to get richer, and the poor continue to get poorer. People don't have homes; many people are homeless. How would you like it if you were homeless, or even worse, your child is now homeless? People around our country and around the world are starving to death when it is another scientific observational truth, we throw away a large percentage of the food we grow in our world. *No* humans should die of starvation and yet our leaders can't seem to figure this out.

Human beings don't have healthcare. Do you know how many people I saw when I had my retinas detached that were sent home to go blind because they didn't have the health insurance to have the surgeries needed to correct it? Many. If you google *detached retinas* it says, not life threatening. How would you like to live without an eye, what about living blind? Being blind when you were able to see your whole life seems pretty life threatening to me, how about you?

People are killing and eating animals for their own enjoyment when we also know another 'scientific observational truth.' Killing and eating animals is a big part of the problem of our current ecosystem that is failing us and leading to the destruction of our planet, Earth. Mother Nature killed over one billion animals in January 2020 in Australia, almost the same time she created coronavirus to rid our planet of millions of human beings. We had a *huge* output of CO_2 everyday worldwide killing our environment, our ecosystem, another 'scientific observational truth." Cigarettes/Cigars (tobacco products) and Jul's available for sale even though we know it kills us and our children and grandchildren *and* it is hurting the environment.

Almost nothing is *made* in the USA today. *Not* the food, not the drugs, not the small wares and the hardware, not our clothes, nothing. I believe we wait until the current government has committed suicide. At that point, we create farms and more farms to put our people back to work in new jobs, all jobs that are created for the benefit of our country's people. All countries will follow us, every country can take care of themselves. Everything is made in the country in which we live and love in. Until we create a new economy, an economy which works for the people we will continue to be working for the rich and greedy men/women who currently are the only ones who are benefiting from our current economy. Unfortunately, all the mega rich kids' life spans are at serious risk. Starving to death worldwide in our future. We need to work together and quickly as our clock to save earth is ticking.

Most companies were non-essential. Bringing them back doesn't make much sense at all, does it?

Synthetic drugs and drug companies continue to be a source of evil. Do you really want to get rid of diabetes or do you want to complain, shoot up with drugs, and then continue to drink Coke and eat pringles for a snack? These drugs should be banned from the market and companies i.e., Johnson and Johnson should be out of business effective immediately. Did you know that over 10% of our population has diabetes and over 60% of our kids today are prediabetic? *NOoodle* (a plant and water-based dough) if eaten everyday cures diabetes. We have food that cures diabetes on the market, but no one is listening. We need to start listening. Have you ever wondered why obese people are usually not seen in old age homes? They eat themselves to death and die of a very painful death. Sugar is the number one cause of addiction and death. Google it, another scientific observational truth. Recycling: we suck at it! Why? Our government sucks at it. Two separate garbage's? No, that is not working. It doesn't work. We need six separates, maybe not on each corner but in NYC on each AVE. One for glass. One of aluminum cans and foil. One for plastic. One for paper and cardboard. One for compost. One of all others, i.e., trash.

Prisons, our systems are not working. Who are the lawbreakers, the guards, or the prisoners or both? Have you ever seen, *Escape from New York?* I saw it when I was young. When I am president, I will be buying islands and shipping all the prisoners to different islands (depending on their crimes). We will drop food and they can fend for themselves. The evil humans can be loaded into the space shuttles Bezos and gang created and we can blast them off to Mars. Beam them up Scotty! Guns; amendment number 2 of the constitution of the USA. It will need to be overturned. It has happened in the past, we overturned the constitution when we wanted to drink alcohol, we can overturn it to protect the many lives of the innocent. We are not our militia, and we don't have the right to bear arms. We clearly have abused that right overtime. The police, just like many in power, are now part of the problem of terror. Is it the CPD or the Latin Kings or both? Maybe today they are a combo kid. 2021 made January 6th a special day in American history, the insurrection. January 6th is also the biggest celebration day for the Latin Kings, 'Three King's Day', the feast of the epiphany. Our innocent children were being murdered day in and day out. Guns to hunt? We won't need anymore because hunting and killing animals to eat is part of the major issue that is causing climate change. Hunting is banned. Animals deserve a right to live in nature.

Schools didn't work. If our children were coming home alive, they may have been coming home with scars that we can't see. Scars from bullying that are forcing the percentages of suicides to skyrocket. Big pharma needs to start explaining themselves to all the parents in the world whose children have been popping singular (aka Montelukast), every day for years now, maybe even decades. Have you seen the show, *13 reasons why?* You should watch it if you haven't. The old saying, "Sticks and stones will break my bones, but names will never hurt me." Total BS. It is our feelings that are weaker than our bones. Today our children are safe at home, being home schooled. I have faith that one day all social media will be banned. Although it was social media that created GENamaZing, GEN Z, it was created for them and not for future generations. Mano y mano, face to face, love thy neighbor. This is the OG way to a great life we love. Social media, bullying, fighting, voicing our opinions doesn't work for humanity. It doesn't work for the word of health and wellness. Again, don't take my word for it, google it. It is another, scientific observational truth, the proof is in the pudding as the saying goes.

Soda companies, juice companies, brands like Gatorade need to be distinguished. Drinking sugar is part of the biggest problem we are facing today as Americans. If we are not slowly dying from diabetes and heart disease and other food borne illnesses, we are paying too much money to enable those of us who are dying slowly. We need to drink water, tea, coffee, and fruit juices made from scratch.

Football is one of America's biggest pastimes. A sport that is so dangerous to watch. Dangerous to play. A sport that gives athletes millions and millions of dollars to beat up each other. A sport that children are loving, and it is aggressive and dangerous. All sports, i.e., Wrestling and boxing that hurt others are not sports, they are inhumane. We are inhumane for making these sports popular. We need to change Football to 'two-hand touch.' Gambling/ Prostitution for me the two go hand in hand. No more…it is dirty, stupid and it prevents a life we love.

It is April 13th, and I am reading a book by Bob Woodward called *Fear*. I started to wonder how we got here as a country. I didn't get through the entire book as it was very upsetting to me. It made me start thinking about past presidents and I started reading all about Ben Franklin for some reason. I believe Ben Franklin was probably the greatest thinker of all time. He was also not the best family man. I really had no idea until today Ben was quite the ladies' man. Nobody is perfect and Ben was no exception. I came across his famous 13 virtues, he writes.

1. Temperance: Eat not to dullness. Drink not to elevation.
2. Silence: Speak not but what may benefit others of yourself. Avoid trifling conversation.
3. Order: Let all things have their places. Let each part of your business have its time.
4. Resolution: Resolve to perform what you ought. Perform without fail what you resolve.
5. Frugality: Make on expense but to do good to others or yourself.
6. Industry: Lose no time. Be always employed in something useful.
7. Sincerity: Use no hurtful deceit. Think innocently and justly. If you speak, speak accordingly. No gossip or blaming others.
8. Justice: Wrong none by doing.
9. Moderation: Avoid extremes, for bear injuries so much as you think they deserve.
10. Cleanliness: Tolerate no uncleanliness in body, clothes, or habitation.

11. Tranquility: Be not disturbed at trifles or at accidents common or unavoidable.
12. Chastity: Rarely use venery (sexual indulgence) but for health or offspring—never to dullness, weakness, or the injury of your own or another's peace or reputation.
13. Humility: Imitate Jesus and Socrates

It is hard for me to believe the amazing vision Ben Franklin had all those many years ago. If we can all accomplish these thirteen virtues daily without fail? One of his famous sayings is, "Life is a kind of chess." Is it really, Ben? I believe this is part of the problem in big business today. Our leaders are playing with our lives as they play to win a chess game. The problem is the pawns are real people with people who love them and many people they love. People are not pawns to be played with as we do in a game of chess. We can't use people in this regard to win the game. We clearly are not winning the game as we play it. The game of life is not winning right now. Our leaders, we must find a new way...a new game. The book *Fear* had me researching past presidents. I wanted to know how we got to this place exactly. I believe to find answers about today, it's important to understand our past. George Washington, our first president. Alexander Hamilton was George's trusted friend and advisor. Together with John Adams, Franklin, Thomas Jefferson they all created the articles of the confederation to secure our rights. The government has arrived. Free independent states dissolved from Britain. George becomes the first president in New York Harbor. Alexander Hamilton says, "Think continentally...let your conversation be without malice or envy…and in all cases of passion admit reason to govern."

I think about all the times in my career with NOoodle. I said passion, my passion. It has been my passion, uncontrollable emotions, that has been my biggest obstacle in business. Passion in government is not allowed. Passion is not in the best interest of our country. Passion is not in the best interest of any business. Emotion equals bad decision making. Passion equals bad judgement. Passion could lead to war. Passion is *not* part of correct government.

I got it now. To govern correctly is to be 100% free of emotion. Emotion is personal. To govern is not about us…it is about them.

Donald Trump…you need…you must remember the words of our first president. George Washington said, "Cunning, ambitions, and unprincipled men will subvert the power of the people. Usurp for themselves the reins of government, destroying afterwards the very engines which has lifted them to unjust domination. These ambitious and unprincipled men were inclined to the passions of the people to assist in their rise to power."

The American people voted Donald Trump in, why? I believe, we, the American people are ruled by our own passions. We are ruled by our own emotions. We as a community, a group, have no control over our passions and emotions. We did this. To see a great and positive change today we must take responsibility that most of us do not have control over our emotions. I believe we need to change the way we think. We need to get out of our own way. We are standing in the way of our own peace and happiness. We are to blame for voting in a known rapist, an evil man. Why?

I believe we voted him in because of our fears, our greed, racism, discrimination. We just kept talking as a country, making each other wrong to make ourselves right. When will we stop talking and start listening? Do all our children and loved ones must die before we start listening? Who wants to die? Who wants to cease to exist? It is 2020, let's take account of what has happened so far this year?

Over one billion animals perished in January. 210 countries confirmed 1,857,310 confirmed cases of coronavirus. 114, 358 deaths confirmed as of April 13th, 2020. I find it interesting a news outlet reported 210 countries confirming covid-19. I thought there are only 195 countries in our world today. I thought 192 countries out of 195 countries are included in the UN. Now we have 210 countries. Humm…these must be the counties who call themselves countries, but they are terrorist organizations calling themselves countries. Exponential growth is defined as, "growth whose rat becomes ever more rapid in proportion to the growing total number in size."

How many more people in our world need to die before we stop talking and start listening? This is not the China-virus as our ill-informed president continues to say. The coronavirus is a virus that has been created by us, by mother nature, by God. God, we, also created the wildfires in Australia and killed over a billion of our godlike creatures. Why? It is obvious to me. We are killing each other, we are killing her, we are killing God. She/he/they/y'all aka God is fighting us back. We are teaching ourselves a lesson. Simply put, if we, humanity, are going to kill her, mother nature, she is going to kill us first. Mother nature, God – she and her will have the final say of who will die, when.

I request today that the reformed party ticket gets back on the ballot in 2024. In honor of Thomas Jefferson, James Madison, Andrew Jackson and all the other good men who represented good women, it is time to take back our independence! We must do what is necessary to save our world. Our Earth, our heaven, heaven on Earth. We must respect mother nature/God. We must have the utmost affinity for them. Together we must decide to concern ourselves with a larger group of people, the United Nations to be exact, all of us, all around the world. The entire human race and all species, all inhabitants, of our planet Earth. It will be decided by an assemblage of people equally divided between men and women. Equality of body, mind, and spirit. Individualism, humanism, universalism. Together we will end the imbalance of human nature. End the eternal struggle between mind and body. End the internal conflict between our neighbors. End the eternal war between God and us because after all, we are all part of God. The time has come for all of humanity to take an Avatarian point of view.

Thomas Jefferson, our third president. Known as the best president who ever lived by many. He said some many famous things, "We hold these truths to be self-evident; that all men and women are created equal." He said, "Our liberty depends on the freedom of the press, and that cannot be limited without being lost." He said, "Nothing can now be believed which is seen in a newspaper. Truth itself becomes suspicious by being but into that polluted vehicle." He said, "I, however, place the economy among the first and most important republican virtues, and public debt as the greatest of dampers to be feared". I wonder how Thomas would feel knowing that the Chinese government basically owns the

American market today. He also said, "I cannot live without a book." Did you know Jefferson had a collection of 6700 books, he eventually sold all his books to our government's library for $23,950. Thankfully because all the original books owned by our new government were lost in the war of 1812.

I copied an article in the news on April 13th, 2020. It read, "*U.S. Perilously close to Meat shortage after major plant closes over coronavirus.*"

I wrote, "*I warned you guys a few weeks ago to stop eating all meat, they say coronavirus is passed through animal meat. Please consider becoming a vegetarian asap.*"

Alex wrote back, "*It doesn't transfer thru food but that is still an awful story.*"

April 17th, "*Kundalini Shakti is so deft in her own creation. Not only does she create but she creates everything upon her own Being. A potter makes pots using clay, but she creates everything out of her own being, within her own being, and upon her own being. Therefore, she is called both translucent and immanent. She is in the universe; she is also beyond the universe. She is within everything, yet she transcends everything also. She is both the womb and the child. What an incredible, infinite play this is! Truly speaking, Shakti is the most precious of all. She is day, and she is night. She is the sun, and she is the moon. She is high tide, and she is low tide. She is loss, and she is gain. She is the power in all that exists and all that does not exist. She is a moment, and she has infinites. She makes the eyes blink, and the lips move. She bestows fortune and misfortune. If you know her, you smile and play her. If you don't know her you live in misery. She must be known.*"

Let's put it this way: She wants to be known. She is the Holy Spirit. She is sacred. She touches all but remains untouched. She sees all but remains unseen. She belongs to everyone, but no one owns her. Without her there is no universe." – Gurumayi Chidvilasananda

Yesterday I woke up very inspired. I was able to sleep till 5:30 am which is a tremendous amount for me lately. Today was the opposite. I woke up early this morning. I didn't sleep much, and I had a horrible lucid dream of a ship I was on that capsized. I was on a ship on the river in downtown Chicago. I was with my son Alex; now we were on the opposite side (width way) and the boat quickly turned over. In my dream I was taken under, and I finally swam up to catch my breath. I quickly swam with all my power and swimmers' strength to his side. I was screaming his name. I instantly knew I had to swim down and find him under the water. I did and I saved him! I woke incredibly relieved it was just a bad dream. I no longer wanted a strained relationship with my oldest son. I wanted him to be toward me more kind, empathic and loving as he seemed to be to everyone else but me. I realized this morning that Alex is perfect exactly the way he is. It is my expectations of his behaviors which is such BS! No more! Ever! This is a *new* day! My son Alex is an incredible human being. Whatever I can do for him always I will do this time without any expectations. I notice today that I am giving up more and more control every day. I see myself clearer and clearer.

April 18th is a great day! I finally slept through the night which has not happened since March 2nd, when my nightmare began. I was stuck here in my 370 square foot apartment. I didn't have any access to a phone. The only person I feel connected to these days is Governor Cuomo as he is constantly talking on the TV in the background. I never intended to spend much time in my studio apartment. After all I moved here for the fun, the action, everything *but* these four small walls. It does have a cute little kitchen, but I absolutely hate the bathroom. The grout in my shower has mold in it. I just can't clean mold out of grout, especially when it was not my creation. I hate showering here. What to do? I know…I am going to get to the root of my dirty shower. I decided to take out the entire glass shower door. It gave me a project to do. I started with the bathroom door and then I took off all the doors of the kitchen. The cabinets were so old and scratched. I spent over $750 on supplies, and I redid my kitchen over the next several days. It was a gift in the making. It gave me a purpose, something to create something to make better, something to do. It has allowed me to have some purpose, remodeling my apartment. I knew it was not allowed to be done in the lease but the way I see it, I was making improvements so they should be happy. Either way I was doing it. During my projects I had some time to reflect on what I was going to do next. I needed to continue to work on projects. Being creative was helping me sleep and each day, I was slowly feeling better. Every day, as I would walk to the hardware store and my cleaners and all the great food stores in my neighborhood, I would walk past so many homeless people. My heart was with them during this time. I was having a very hard time through the pandemic. I knew it was nothing compared to what the homeless in NYC were experiencing. *We must never give up on people*, I thought. It is our jobs, all our jobs, as leaders to NOT give up those who fall on hard times. We must always help them. I believe most of the homeless that I have met over the past month want to work. They want to add value into the world they just lost their way. They need a way back to life…back to reality…they need a job!

Chapter 5

Sunday Funday? Not Today. Today Sunday Is a Day of Rest and Worship

I worship humanity today. I always worshiped humanity which is why I choose to study Human communications in college. I wanted to have a career that involved working with people. I thought learning the way humans communicate would be a great place to start. I am not sure it was until today I understood why I had such an affinity for people. Today I believe with all my heart humanity is the highest power. Humanity is the top layer of God.

"If you put a crystal in a fire, it cracks inside. If you keep it in the fire, it continues to crack into tinier and tinier parts. The crystal is still whole but, on the inside, it becomes fragmented and reflects the light like a diamond in many facets. In the same way, as the inner awakening takes place, the fire of consciousness burns away all impurities, all negatives. You are still in the body, but inside, everything becomes consciousness, everything becomes light.

"In the crystal, you can see all the colors sparkling, and it is the same with this body. As it goes on burning in the fire of love, the fire of truth, it becomes consciousness, nothing but consciousness." – Gurumayi Chidvilasananda

It is humanity which is God's highest creation. We are his and hers (God) number one creation. We are so intelligent it is hard to understand how doctors can be so incredibly smart. How artists can see landscapes and faces in so many dimensions. How lawyers can understand the law language the way it was written. How mothers instinctively know what is wrong with their sick child. How one person, Jeff Bezos, can disrupt the entire marketplace as he created (what I believe to be) the first true spider monopoly in our world. Specially today I am worshiping all mothers throughout our world.

I have felt so alone during this time, sheltered in place by myself I decide to go through all the schoolwork, pictures, cards, everything I had from the years of raising my two boys. I have cried and cried and cried over the last thirty days. I have experienced so much sadness for myself and humanity. I came across so many of the Mother's Day cards I received over the years from my boys. This one from Jake stuck out. I believe he was eighteen years old when he wrote this. He writes, "*Happy Mother's Day, Mom! You are an incredible and wonderful person (being). You light up the space in a positive way when you choose to. You have been a great mom and continue to be that person in my life. I love you and this day is only one day that we recognize you. All days that I live you are recognized. Jake.*"

Today's latest news topics.

Bloomberg, "*Florida saw a record number of new cases on Friday, the same day Governor Ron DeSantis gave the green light to return to local beaches. Meanwhile, Trump said some states (like Hawaii, Wyoming, and Utah) are* ready to reopen. *But the states say they don't actually meet the administration's criteria to do so.*"

The Washington Post's headline, "*Covid-19 is rapidly becoming America's leading cause of death. From April 6 to 12, it killed more people than cancer, accidents, strokes, and Alzheimer's do in a normal April week, outpacing everything except heart disease.*"

Los Angeles Times had this to lead with today. "*Trump defended a series of protests against stay-at-home restrictions, saying some governors had overreacted in their efforts to fight the pandemic-though those efforts were based on the advice of his own administration.*"

The Wall Street Journal decided to go global today. The biggest story started with, "*Europe is slowly emerging from its coronavirus lockdown. Country by country (and) in some cases, storefront by storefront), health authorities are selecting when and where commercial life can begin again. 'It's a hard-mental shift,' said an official from the Czech Republic.*"

Now to the Big Questions of the day. Wall Street Journal, "*Will warmer weather slow the virus's spread?*" FiveThirtyEight asks, "*Why did the world shut down for the coronavirus but not Ebola or Sars?*" Wired asks us, "*We know what COVID-19 does to your lungs. But what does it do to your brain?*"

Today I went for a long walk past the beautiful community garden on my street, 89th between Columbus and Amsterdam. I stopped to take in the most amazing array of tulips I have ever seen, except for when I lived in Amsterdam in 2015. My new friend, although I may not ever see her again is Toni. I met her in the garden. She was staring at the tulips, and I noticed she was crying. I said, "*Hi*, are you okay?" thru my masked covered face.

She said, "My husband just died. We were married for fifty years. He died of complications due to covid. I am all alone during this time and we can't even have a funeral and sit shiva due to covid."

My heart bled for hers. At that moment I felt blessed that I didn't have to deal with the loss that Toni is dealing with now.

As a vegetarian I wasn't eating any meat or fish, I was eating only the bi products of meat and fish. I was eating so much Caviar. Almost every other day I would walk to Zabar's to buy some salmon Caviar. I had also declared I was never going to purchase anything (if I could help it) that was not made in the USA. I knew we must stop moving on a macro level to save our planet. On a micro level, we needed to move so much more. Many of us in our country are not moving their bodies enough. I believe this is a huge part of the sickness in our country today. I started researching science for environment policy. I didn't stop eating meat and fish because of my own personal health. I stopped eating meat and fish because it was the only thing, I could do to help our planet in the short term. Luckily for me, after lots of research there are nine species of fish, if harvested correctly, are great for our ecosystem. I can start eating Tuna and White fish again. I can eat lobster and most shellfish!

April 20th, 2020, "A seeker's attitude toward life cannot be passive. You are not just sitting there laid back, watching the drama of life unfold. Just the opposite. Nourished by the ongoing experience of the Shakti, you experience neartedly in God's creation, but at the same time, you in detached and never forget that all this is God's r ." – Gurumayi Chidvilasananda

Today marks Monday, the start of the work week. For those of you who don't know what Shakti means you are not alone. I just looked it up on google because I didn't know what it meant either. Shakti, "Energy, ability, strength, effort, and power. Capability is the primordial cosmic energy and represents the dynamic forces that are thought to move through the entire universe."

Detach...detachment, that word. Wow...a very hard concept indeed. In this regard, Gurumayi is referring to the third definition of detachment. "The action or process of detaching from separation." I believe this is the hardest thing us human beings can excel at. We are said to be attached to those who we love. What happens when these people we love most, our children, our significant others, our parents don't agree with our choices? What happens if our behaviors, for whatever reasons, most people think are weird, crazy, not normal? I know what usually happens. They leave us alone. They don't call, they don't visit, they detach. They break all ties with us. Why? I believe it is the ego that makes our loved ones leave us. Ego...a person's sense of self-esteem/self-importance/self-worth.

I wonder why I was meant to lose my mind. Maybe I needed to lose it to gain so much? I completed many masterclasses during the nights I was not able to sleep. I decided to write Neil DeGrasse Tyson a note, his class completely inspired me. I googled his company and on the contact page I wrote this: *"Neil...what is science really saying? I am listening, please speak into my listening. I believe I am only one of the millions and millions of people around the world who are listening and want to know what you believe to be true regarding the 'scientific point of view of what is occurring today. Thank you in advance for acknowledging my request to you. I would love it if you would come to Shepherds Fountain in Central Park. We are there every day when the sun is shining or at least it is not raining. Great artists sing and we spread out and do yoga and protocol fitness. I sing and dance on my head and show others how to dance and sing on their heads. I would love, love, love to meet you in Central Park. Thank you for your masterclass, it was great! Chef Terri Rogers."*

"She is the power of becoming, released out of the eternal Being and expressing Herself through all names, all forms, and all changes that we call the world. Indeed, she is the most magnificent power. Sri Kundalini Shakti—of the supreme reality.

And one who gives Shaktipat Diksha, initiation is a GURU." – Swami Muktananda

A Guru? Me? A Guru? Could that be? I did what I would normally do in this situation. It happens to me often in my life. In different situations I advance regarding the relevance of myself.

Me the ID…the ego…my ego. The total circumference including everything inside of me and everything on the outside of me.

It has been overtime that I have tried and tried over and over to access 'Who I am.' Who I be…as in the action of being? Who I want to become? I am pretty sure many of you who are reading this ask yourself questions about self-inquiry often. Getting to know oneself is a great thing, it

.t doesn't happen overnight, in fact, if we are lucky .aappen in our lifetime, decades before we die. My .ke believes true happiness exists only the day we die. He .s GEN Z aka GENamaZing. I think he is right with one exception. Those gurus who truly live in the moment. Live each moment as a gift as if tomorrow may never come. Today as I write this, I am fifty-one years old. I believe that I am middle-aged. Meaning I would die at one hundred and two years old. I believe I will not be dying that young.

Young I say, yes young. Why do I believe I will live past one hundred and two today? It comes down to what I have learned from being a leader in the future of food. It comes down to what I have learned in my journey to get to this place of knowledge. It comes down to being a sponge, a philomath, and sucking up all the great advice from the many mentors I have had in my life. It comes down to understanding that no matter how much I know today it is a speck of what there is to know. It comes down to what I recently learned from a kind; genius soul named Neil DeGrasse Tyson. He makes his points clear and easy to remember. Recall is very important if you want to become the first female president of the greatest country in the world, the United States of America.

Yes, this is the situation that I have put myself into. I believe today it is not only my calling but my duty to run for the highest and most powerful office in the world. I believe I will live long, maybe even the longest a woman has ever lived. It would also mean that I would live longer (or as long) as any human being in the world would live. Why is this important to me? I believe when we pass on, we leave our love, our legacy of love behind. The way we create a big, huge, and powerful legacy of love is by working hard over time on Earth. The more time we have on our amazing planet the chances go up regarding the positive impact we have on humanity.

Neil taught me the term, 'Objective Truth.' Neil is famous because of his genius as it relates to his hard work overtime in the field of science. He is a 'Mad Scientist', and I am mad about him. I tend to fall in love (not in a romantic way) with my mentors. I am so inspired by them for teaching me something new about life and about myself I create a big, big love. I don't believe I am unique in this way. After all, who doesn't fall in love with their best teachers in life? We love our teachers and mentors. I believe this is what nurture means. Why do we love our parents so much? They are our biggest teachers. I believe our teachers are not always positive or inspiring at times. How could they be, they, we…are human beings. I have faith some of you are now thinking about your favorite teachers and you may be saying, "I don't love him, or I didn't love her." It is true; sometimes, often, our best teachers are the ones who broke our heart.

I must stop myself here and let you know that today I don't believe *anyone,* and anything broke our own heart. Why not? It is simply because our heart, our hearts, belong to us. They are our hearts. Your heart is your heart. My heart is my heart. His, her, and y'all's heart is y'all's heart. When we say, "He broke my heart. Why did he break my heart?" is simply another way of us not taking responsibility for our choices, our actions? I find it amazing how human beings; we are all wired the same way. We are wired to *not* take responsibility for the results we get in life. Instead, we

89

blame others, we blame everyone and anyone just so we can 'look good' to our friends, our family and most importantly, ourselves.

The truth, weather we choose to believe it, our hearts belong to us, and they are our hearts to break. We create the situations in our lives. We create love affairs. We create the expectations that often lead to disappointment. We break *our* hearts. If we are lucky our hearts get broken over and repeatedly throughout life. One of my very first mentors, Werner Erhard said, "The bigger the breakdown, the greater the breakthrough…" I have lived through tremendous breakdowns already. A chapter 7 after great success. I guess the stress of chapter 7 was so big for me both my retinas decided to detach from my brain. My real-life hero Dr. Blaire didn't have the answers either In November 2016 when my first retina decided to detach from my brain. When I asked him how my retina could detach spontaneously, he replied, "It is just very bad luck."

At the time I had just gotten back from completing a 420-mile 6-day bike ride in the Spanish Pyrenees. At 46, I was a size two and in the best shape of my life.

No, it wasn't just very bad luck. I had a Merina IUD in me and neither one of us were privy of the many side effects. One of the side effects is deterioration of retinas. Who knew? Certainly not the doctors. If our gynecologists knew about the 'Merina IUD pseudo cerebri brain tumor', Bayer aka Johnson and Johnson would be forced to recall the five million Merina IUD's currently in distribution in the bodies of five million woman around the world today.

Werner was and is correct, "The bigger the breakdown, the greater the breakthrough." I have faith a big breakthrough is coming for the innocent whose lives have been greatly harmed by Johnson and Johnson.

I have been known to not love computers. I believe I work best, old school. When it comes to my cooking, I use my hands and a knife. I get the small wares out sometimes but not often. Did you know OG stands for the original? As proclaimed, "Mother of dragons (my boys 23 and 21 years) I would have to agree with my sons' friends. I may be the coolest mom ever. I believe I would be tied with many of the other billions of moms reading this. We are all '*cool*' in our own way, cool is when we care about people. *Cool* is being able to be transparent and honest in our love and communication with our children."

I think about the twenty-one years we lived in our house on 38 Berkshire Lane, In Lincolnshire Il. I don't regret a thing although if I could like a do-over. I believe as mothers and fathers who have already raised our children, we would all want a do-over. I believe with all my heart the do-overs are when we are lucky and gifted our grandchildren and great grandchildren. Although I made lots of mistakes in my past, I can honestly tell you I have no regrets. I believe 'to regret' is to hold on to our past mistakes, kind of like holding on to baggage. Bags are heavy and they weigh on us. I find it interesting most of my wealthy friends and family have *huge* closets of expensive bags and clothing they never wear. The perfect example, example of 'baggage.' Imagine how much joy they would get if they gifted all those 'things' to people who don't have one bag to put their belongings in. I know they would get great joy, but it is not my place to force outcomes on other people. I believe these are the situations we need to just be. When I force outcomes onto other people and into the world I always fail. I lose the person I love. I lose when it comes to a positive outcome. When I look back the outcomes are always outcomes that I wanted to avoid, and yet they happened.

Hindsight is 20-20. I would love a do-over with the knowledge and wisdom I have acquired but that is not real, it is not life. Instead, I write my books. I write for all of you who are still young and those of you who are like me, middle aged. Also, for those of you who are older, and chances are wiser than I. We become wise when we realize that although we may know a lot, we know nothing in comparison to what there is to know. I term this as, "We don't know what we don't know." We are always saying in life when something happens, "It is what it is."

Yes, that is a true statement. I usually add the following… "It is what it is, *and* it is not what it is not. It seems more understood to me when I add, 'It's not what it is not.'" I think for me, in my life, although I accept what something is, I tend to create what it is into something that it is not. As you already know I am a Pisces female, we are known to be dreamers. According to mythical history we are referred to as the mother of dragons. I love being a dreamer. It has gotten me in trouble in my past and I wouldn't change that about me. As James Dean said, "Dream as if you will live forever, live as you will die today." Ironically, he died young, but his quote stands the test of time. We need to dream big *and* act (work hard over time) every day if we want to see our dreams come true.

When the Parkland shootings happened in January of 2018, I was recovering from my second detached retina (my fifth eye surgery) at my home on 38 Berkshire Lane, in Lincolnshire. I am a very lucky woman. If this was 1975, I would be blind by the time I reached my 50th birthday. Instead, thanks to my genius doctors, surgeons, and nurses today I have two 'bionic eyes.' They are as bionic as eyes can be. I have 20/30 vision without correction and with correction 20/20 vision.

I was distraught about the shooting and the reality of them being a part of the new normal. I created the domain that day, *GENamaZing.com* for my boys. I knew in my heart It was going to be the Alex and Jake generation that would change the world to become a better and healthier place to live. My boys, I would say I was part of the village that raised them. They are two of the sweetest kids I know. They are kind to others, kind to strangers and they both have big, big hearts. Giving birth was surreal for me. It was *God*-like. It was a magical and mystical ride. I know every parent, well at least every mom, will agree with me. We are so blessed. All of us mothers and fathers who are parents. If you are not a parent, I have faith after you finish reading my book, you will be inspired to have children. I don't believe having children means you have to give birth. Having children is making the choice to adopt a child, better yet, children. To *adopt*—verb; legally take (another child) and bring him/her/them up as your own. The love we can give and receive from our new child is truly, *God.* There is nothing bigger and better than the love a parent feels for our children. Call me crazy but I really can't relate to anyone who has the ability (financially) who doesn't choose to have a child, either naturally or adopted. My judgement of them overtakes me. I automatically believe that any human being (female and male) who makes the decision to *not* have a child in some way is being either selfish or they are scared.

To be scared is easier to get through than being selfish. Those of you who are scared I say this; It is okay to be scared, it is human nature. Especially when our parents may have not done a great job (from our point of view) with us. I will quote William Shakespeare in hopes that after you read this you won't be afraid to accept the number 1 gift from *God*, the love we have for our child/children.

"Our worries (fears) are traitors and make us lose the good we might not get by fearing to attempt." – William Shakespeare. Okay…*poof*…now you are not afraid anymore because fear is the root of all evil. We must be able to stare fear in the face by doing…acting. A great life is one that creates lots of actions for us each day. It is in the giving where life truly exists.

The second reason you have decided to not become a parent. Selfish; adjective (of a person, action, or motive) lacking consideration for others; concerned chiefly with one's own personal profit or pleasure. Are you selfish? Do you see yourself as selfish? No one else matters, it is for you to see this for yourself regarding yourself. We all have selfishness in us. We all have demons, and we all have bad habits. We need to start accepting each other. We need to start being less judgmental of those we love and those we don't love. We need to start taking responsibility for the ugly that is in each one of us.

Today is April 25th, 2020. It is a beautiful day here in NYC, the epicenter of *love*. Today I get to go outside and breathe in the fresh air. I get to hear the birds singing. I get to breath. I get to go to the store and buy produce and cook for my neighbors tonight.

I recently started cooking every night for several of my neighbors who prior to coronavirus were strangers. In fact, I don't recall ever seeing their faces and they sleep every night less than fifty feet away from where I sleep. They saved me in a way. It has been several weeks now that I first started hearing the drums beat at 7:00 pm. I was suffering from what is termed today as, 'isolation anxiety.' It was the very day I flew back from Chicago. That night, I believe April 3rd *God* sent me a gift. A gift in the form of people beating on drums. It was 7:00 pm to 7:03, three minutes when all of NYC came up and made noise for the first responders. I came out in a fog, my neighbor, Louie remembers when I first came out and crossed the street to talk to him. He had no idea what I was going through and thankfully they were there for me. Cowboy Joe (who you can catch nightly on the Stephan Colbert show), his very pregnant wife Lauren (she is due next month, yippie a baby I can love from a distance) and Jane.

Our great city, New York City, was the first city to be impacted in our country. Of course, it was! I believe mother nature created it to be this way. Leaders need to be on the front line, always. Leaders need to lead by example. I loved living in Chicago for twenty-eight years, raising my children and creating a career for myself in the future of food. The people are great and easy going. They are different from New Yorkers. I know why. New Yorkers are the leaders of the free world. *We* are the standard. Ellis Island is Ellis Island for a reason, and it is situated in NYC.

We are the trendsetters; we are children of the original hippies. We are the hipsters. Kids raised with parents who celebrated all holidays except for Easter. Let's face it…no one from NYC believed Jesus was going to come back again. He was going to rise from the water and bring us to the promised land? No…my mom told us we were going to be recreated into a tree or a cat or a bird when we died. Okay…we also got to watch *Roots* when my siblings and I were 4, 6, 10 years old. We were raised with Kunta Kinte, The Beatles, Willy Randolph, Stephanie mills, John Denver and of course, good old' Stevie Wonder. If he could sing and play the piano blind, then we knew it was possible to do anything and everything. Our world was ours to get and our parents molded my siblings and I to become empath leaders.

Today the world has come to know NYC as the epicenter of coronavirus, aka the epicenter of death. Most of the people I know who had second homes were 'running scared' out of NYC. They are still gone. Every day, if I want the best slice of pizza for $3 a slice, I can have one. I can have a great bagel with butter for $2 and see happy faces. It has been these happy faces, the faces of my cleaners, my local Duane Reade, everyone at Chase bank, our local post office, the liquor stores, the corner vegetable markets, Zabar's, Broadway farms, the paint stores, the appliance stores, the pickle stores, the fish markets, Barneys Greengrass, you name it they are here to help us through this time of great change. Through this time of rebuilding with, by, and through love.

Chapter 6

I am a Chef, not a Baker. Baker What?

In May 2019, there was no shortage of homeless/mentally ill/drug addicts in need of food. When the man gave me the check for my food, I realized I didn't have anything on me. I left all my bags under the bridge along with my phone since it was giving me all the trouble with directions. I told him I promised I would be back later that day to pay. I guess I was having heat exhaustion but wasn't aware of it at the time. If I were thinking straight, I never would have left my phone and wallet in my bag. I must have already been in a state of delirium. I headed back toward the hotel and stopped into a blood bank to get a map. No maps so the lady at the counter created a handwritten one for me to follow to the hotel. I finally arrived sometime around 1:00 pm. I was asking for water and then I had to sit down. I finally checked in. My reservation was prepaid thru Hotel tonight. They asked me for my license, which I didn't have. I requested to be let into my room and I would call for help to retrieve my license. They said they couldn't do it.

The next thing I remember, I was starting to have an itch in my throat. Over the years, I realized that when I feel stressed, my throat, eyes and ears would start itching. It was a signal that I was about to have an anaphylaxis attack. My EpiPen and my Benadryl were in my bag with my phone and license. The manager asked if I needed help and at that moment, my throat started itching and my mouth started closing. I felt an attack coming on, I said yes. I sat down and started to breathe and meditate and the itching seemed to stop. The next thing I remember was a police officer came into the hotel and said he needed to take me outside. He escorted me out of the hotel and back into the 100-degree heat. The firemen were taking my vitals and asking me a lot of questions. All I remember was begging the police officer for some water. It must have been around 2:30 pm at this time. I get into the ambulance. I remember I thought the ambulance guy was Tim Ferris. I was completely delirious and according to the hospital report, I was saying crazy things.

In the emergency room at Sarasota Memorial, I don't remember much except the nurses were talking about Donald Trump. No one asked me for a contact name or my name or anything. I remember a lot of talking and laughing and a lot of nurses, techs, etc. The next thing I remember was a shot in my right arm, which lasted a few seconds and then the most painful shot I have ever gotten in my life in my left arm. The pain from the shot seemed to go on forever and I remember wincing in pain. The hospital records show that I was drugged with a mood relaxant 2 mg in my right. The painful shot in my left arm was 5 mg of Haldol, which is given to psychopaths. I believe I woke up about 16 hours later feeling like a drugged zombie. I think it was around 10:00 am the next day.

Where am I? I was in a room with two beds and a big black woman from Africa who was bouncing on her bed facing the wall. I said in a quiet voice, "Hello, where am I?" She didn't respond; she just kept bouncing. I looked down at myself and I am in a hospital gown. I feel completely wasted. I lay there for about 15 minutes until the nurse named Calle came in. She bent down by my bedside, and I asked her, "Where I am?"

She said, "You voluntarily check yourself into Bayside, you volunteered for a Baker Act. (The Baker Act is a Florida law that enables families and loved ones to provide emergency mental health services and temporary detention for people who are impaired because of a mental illness.)

"Baker act, baker what?" Then I got it and I said, "Oh! Hell, no!" From what I remember, I must have been suffering from heat exhaustion/delirium. I thought I was on the verge of an anaphylaxis attack. "This is a big mistake. I had heat exhaustion/delirium and you guys drugged me!" I told her.

She said, "You will need to see the doctor. She will have to sign your release papers, but since you are here voluntarily, it shouldn't be an issue." She said the doctor would come around 3:00 pm. I went outside to the recreation room. I felt completely drugged in an area where the rest of the completely drugged people hang out. It's a room where they have one small TV and they feed you all your meals. I sit down. As soon as I do, a frail sweet woman comes and sits down next to me. She is wearing a T-shirt with the Beatles song lyric, "All you need is love." Dixie is her name. She appears to me to be in good health. She tells me she is 89 and I told her she looked great. She whispers and writes me notes that they are drugging her against her will. She says bad things happen here at night. She says they are mean. She says they won't let us touch or hug each other and asks me if she could hug me. I say sure and she hugs me, and I see the guards (nurses?) are giving us dirty looks.

Next, I meet Karen. She is bald and crying hysterical. She seems like a complete mess, a basket case. She looks about 70 and is crying, saying they took her wig away. She is begging me to ask them for a new wig for her. I told her I would. Then Susan from New York comes over in a wheelchair. I can tell from her legs that she suffers from diabetes. She is a true New Yorker with a tough outside and a sweet and strong inside. Dixie tells me Susan can be mean, but she is nice; she said I will like her. Susan was a tuff cookie from New York City who is probably around 65. She suffers from a bad case of diabetes and is almost blind. She is kind and tough and has a great sense of humor, like a true New Yorker. Sarah is the last female. Sarah looks like a strung-out junkie. She is gone, not there, not at all. She is always smiling, and she doesn't say much but she is sweet, and you can tell she has had a rough-and-tough life. I have never in my life spent time with someone who looked as drugged as Sarah did. I watched as each woman was given hard narcotics. I heard the mention of lithium, benzos, and Percocet. I was just watching and thinking about what Dixie told me a few hours ago, that they drugged patients.

They were drugging her, and she didn't want to be drugged but they made her take the drugs. I watched them go from being crazy strung-out junkies to crazy buzzed and happy junkies. My doctor finally shows up around 3:00 pm. I would call her the gatekeeper to hell. This doctor didn't have a caring bone in her body. One day she may have cared about people, but those days were long gone. She struck me as someone who became a doctor so she can control people and not in a positive way. We meet for five minutes, not even. She tells me I had a psychotic episode. She tells me I said I was the mother of dragons, and I was going to be a better president than Donald Trump. I told her that I must have been joking. It was a bad joke. She gave me a dirty look and said, "What would you like? Lithium or benzos?"

I told her, "The hospital already drugged me to get me in here. I don't need or want any more drugs."

She said, "If you refuse treatment, then I will change your chart from a voluntary admittance to involuntary."

I said, "I was drugged. I was delirious from heat exhaustion, and they misdiagnosed me in the emergency room. Please Google me, I am not crazy, I am a businesswoman. I own *NOoodle*."

She said,'' If you don't take the drugs, you will be here indefinitely."

"I will stay in the psych ward, but I won't taking any drugs from you."

She said, "You're staying the night," and walked out of the room.

After the doctor left, I went back to my room and cried for about 30 minutes. I tried to talk to my roommate Yolanda, but she was a mute and just kept bouncing on the bed facing the wall. I couldn't understand what was happening to me. At that moment, I became very faithful about this experience. I knew I was in there because for some reason, God wanted me to see what was happening here. Less than a mile away from where I lived, this hospital was drugging people against their will. I had to come to terms I was staying here for the night. I was afraid because Dixie told me bad things happen here at night. They served dinner at 4:00 pm. I asked to go outside, and they allowed me to do so. I waited at least an hour for the tech to let me go outside for some air. It was a hot box with fencing all over it and a closed in roof. It was so depressing it was even hard to stay out there. I just was holding back tears. I went back inside and now everyone is nice and toasted from all the drugs they took after dinner. My brain is slowly coming back to normal. Around 10 o'clock, we go to our rooms. I try to fall asleep, but I hear screaming from the dark hallways.

The night was awful. I just remember that I was so scared of Yolanda that I wanted to keep my door open. Across the hallway was Dixie and Susan. and Susan kept screaming to leave the light on. Every 15 minutes, the techs would come down the dark hallway and shine the black light into our rooms and faces. I managed to fall asleep for a few hours' unit at 1:00 am, it was like an alarm went off in my brain and I got up. I am seeing Dixie, Susan and Karen crying and screaming at the guards to get away. They are giving them pills. Karen is crying about her wig. I am just standing in my doorway making sure these women were not being raped or worse. I was basically up all night. It felt as if I was in the movie *One Flew over the Cuckoo's Nest*. I was reminded of the *Terminator 2: Judgment Day*, when Lisa Hamilton is in the psych ward because she believes in what she believes, and everyone else thinks she is crazy. I found it interesting that my whole adult life people would say I looked like the woman in *Terminator 2*, and now I was living part of the character's life. The nurses would come into our room and check Yolanda's vitals. They asked to check my vitals. I declined each time. I said every time, "No, I am fine. My vitals are fine."

Thank God, I made it through the night. I woke up and I am still in the hospital gown. I was wondering what happened to my lucky bracelet. Where are my clothes? I asked the nurse. I told her I had some Oakley pants and an Under Armor shirt. She gets my clothes and I get dressed. I wondered if I was getting out of here today. The nurse Calle says the doctor changed my chart from voluntary to involuntary; it's up to her. I then did something that I really didn't want to do based on where my relationship was at the time with my mom. My mom was the only number I knew by heart, I didn't have many friends in Florida except my dear friend Jan and Frank. Frank was gone, so I called my mom. I told her I was Baker Acted. She told me that unless I take the drugs the doctor wants to give me, I wouldn't get out of there. She said she was ill and couldn't get out of bed. She said she would send Mike (my stepdad), during visiting hours. I told the nurses that my dad was going to be here to check me out. That was the very first time in all my life that I called him Dad. I didn't want to confuse the doctors and say stepdad. He shows up with a smirk on his face.

We sit down. He looked at me like I was crazy and said, "Terri, you got Baker Acted."

I said, "I know I did."

Then the nurse comes over and says, "Hi, your Terri's dad." He corrects her and says he's a stepdad. I knew right then that calling the two of them was the biggest mistake. I should have known better, and I said goodbye to Mike and went back to my room.

My complete medical records show that my stepfather said I was acting crazy lately and that they should keep me there for more testing. I didn't know he said that until I was able to read the full medical report the following week. My mom said some things about me that were also very negative. Mike told them to keep his conversations about me private, as he wanted to stay on my good side, the report said. I am not sure what was worse being falsely committed or reading what some of my parents had to say about me. They said so many private things to strange doctors and nurses who were holding me captive against my will. Yes, it was true my mom and stepfather have been going through a very hard time lately because my mom's and Mikes's youngest son's behavior change over the past decade. Nick literally checked out of life. She brought up his mental illness in my hospital reports. I have never been prescribed a Xanax in my life. My parents were being seen for a while now by a psychiatrist because of their ongoing relationship issues with Nick, my half-brother.

It was dinnertime and the hospital food was surprisingly good. After dinner, it was visiting hours. I got Jan's phone number from my stepdad. They are friends, too. Jan came to visit. Dixie was so happy all day because she told me her family was coming to visit. Her daughter was so mean to her 89-year-old mom. I found out that her daughter packed Dixie a nice bag with a lot of clothes and sent her into this place, where they drugged this poor woman around the clock. Dixie's husband, daughter's husband and son came in and talked to Dixie. She is crying and begging them to take her home. Her uncaring unloving and uncompassionated daughter leaves in a huff.

Jan enters and I give him a hug. We sit down and the next thing I know, Dixie starts screaming and her family can't control her. She is begging them to take her home, they wrestle with her to get away and they leave feeling terribly embarrassed. They left a fragile, elderly woman crying on the floor. Jan and I just looked at each other and he said sorry they took the pizza I got you away at the front desk. Apparently, you're not allowed to bring food in here. That day, I noticed two new people, two guys. One was grossly overweight, about 50 and couldn't move his legs in the wheelchair without swearing and without help from the techs. He had a terrible case of diabetes, and his feet and legs were rotting away. They were giving him Percocet as he was clearly in pain.

The other new character was a 20-year-old male kid who looked clean cut but wasn't at all. He seemed happy and content to be there. I didn't pay much attention to him on Sunday. I was trying my best to keep to myself. Around 8:00 pm, the nurses were playing *Name That Tune* with the patients. Most of us had one thing in common. We didn't want to be in there. Calle, my nurse, told me on day one that she recognized me from the Arcos Residences. I told her I lived there, and she told me she lived there, too. Now I see Calle almost every day walking her dog. I told her yesterday to get a new job because she is a good nurse and what they are doing there is not only illegal but unjust and criminal. That night in Bayview, she told me to mind my own business and not help anyone who needed or asked for my help. If I did that tonight, then most likely I would be able to go home after the 72 hours was up, which was tomorrow afternoon.

I went to my room at 10:00 pm I tried to converse with Yolanda before going to bed. She just ignored me and continued to face the dead wall and bounce up and down. I tried to go to sleep but Yolanda was distracting me, so I asked the techs if I can move rooms. They said sure. I went into a room with Karen. The room felt safer but had a huge aroma of pee. Karen was so happy now that she got a wig. It wasn't the wig she came in with, but a new wig with long hair and she was touching her hair the entire time. I finally asked why she was here. She said she was about to take a butcher knife and stick it in her belly. She was so lonely and had nothing to live for. Instead, she told her neighbor what she was planning to do, and they Baker Acted her because she was a danger to herself. When in my life have, I ever been a danger to myself or others? Never.

Fear of an anaphylaxis attack and asking for medical help is different. Who was paying for all these mentally sick people to now become mentally sick drug addicts? Note to self, research it when I get out of here. I finally went to sleep and thankfully this time, it was uneventful.

I awoke with an amazing sense of excitement. I am getting out. I am being liberated. I am alive. I get to go home and work on *NOoodle* again. I head down to the main room for breakfast. This time, I am hungry. I am smiling and it is Monday. To my surprise, the new staff, not the graveyard shift, is happy and inspired. I thought to myself I really got to see the worst of this place by being here on the weekend, the second and third and fourth shifts that no one wants. After breakfast, this nice male nurse told me they had a special meeting about me, and he was sure I was going to be out of here today. I just needed to wait until the doctor (the same awful woman) came to sign the release forms. I was so thankful. I did whatever I could that morning to help in the main room. I even started cleaning up chairs with special wipes for the nurses as all the chairs were sticky. I called my friend Jan and told him to please come and get me. They said I would be out by noon, and it was now about 11:00 am in the morning. Jan said he would be over around 1:00 pm to get me. I said perfect by that time the crazy doctor will be around to see her patients and she will set me free. She came around 2:00 pm and I had to meet with her and the sweet new nurse on duty. The doctor told me that because I am 50 and this was my first psychotic episode in my life, she is going to sign the papers to release me. I thanked her. In my mind, I hated the site of her controlling, abusive nature. I hated her and everything she stood for. She gave the word 'doctor' a terrible name—and I hope one day her license is revoked. After she signed my release papers, I thanked her, and she left to make her other rounds. She went into Susan's room. A minute later, the doctor leaves and I hear Susan yell, "What kind of doctor are you? All you want to do is drug me. Where did you get your license? Are you sure you're a real doctor?" Then I saw the gatekeeper from hell walk out of Susan's room with a big smile on her face. She said, "Yes, I am a real doctor, and you will continue to stay here." With a big smile on her face as she walked past me. I hear Sue moaning and screaming.

The techs just shake their head. Sue is her own worst enemy. In here, you must shut your mouth and do the time. In here, you must pretend that your crazy evil doctor is right, and you are wrong. In here, nothing matters. Here, your liberties are taken away. Here, no one cares. Here, you are committed. In here, you are nothing. Here, you are crazy. Here, you are meaningless. In here, the entire system, (the doctors, the nurses, the therapists, the techs, the Baker Act judges, the lawyers, and the janitors), they are all part of a very broken system. They are all paid to turn a blind eye so they can keep their jobs and continue to be part of the terrible corruption that continues to exist in Florida because of the Baker Act.

I am going to get home and then find my car keys to retrieve all my baggage that I left underneath the bridge on Friday. I finally got discharged. Prior to my discharge, I said goodbye to the women who were still in there. Dixie said her family was coming to get her. I really hope so; she didn't deserve to be there. She has a terrible daughter but other than that she is a blessed lady. She may be a bit senile, but she is not a mental patient. They gave me my lucky bracelet. I doubled my hospital socks, and I was going to walk home. Jan came and left so I had no choice but to walk home. The nurse gave me someone else's flip-flops. I took them and checked out the worst experience of my life thus far.

As soon as I left the mental institution, I bumped into the gun and ammunition store. I just stood there in a frozen silence. This is how we are doing it. We, the American people, the taxpayers, are paying for the homeless to come into Florida's hospitals because of a mentally ill law called the Baker Act. The law needs to be overturned. The very last day of my stay, I decided to be a part of group therapy. In the group was that 20-year-old clean-cut looking young man. When the social worker asked us what we were going to do when we go out, he said he was going to leave this country because America was the most screwed up and unfair country there is. I couldn't help but notice the large Confederate flag tattoo on his arm. When I was walking home and staring at the gun store, it all came rushing into my brain at once. Our government is creating the worst terrorism there is right here at home.

Parkland is in Florida and this 20-year-old looks like he could be the next man to murder our children. We are paying for doctors and nurses in Florida to drug the mentally ill. All those abandoned by parents or children and the innocent people like Dixie who may have grown to be a nuisance to us. It is a tragedy on so many levels. I walked home and thankfully; I have a leasing office which was opened. I told them I couldn't find my key fob and to please let me into my apartment. They did and I took my spare car keys and headed out to find my bags. I drove into the vicinity where I thought they were. It took me about 30 minutes and then I knew exactly where I left them. I retrieved my bags, and everything was in there except my car keys and fob, which I replaced the next day. I drove home very happy. I felt so lucky I found my bags and headed home for a relaxing sleep in my own bed.

Phillip calls telling me he is home from his Macon Georgia Trip and wants to come and retrieve all his belongings. When he showed up, he couldn't even look in my eyes. He was still so mad at me. He had no idea what I just went through and for now, I wanted to keep it that way. He packed the rest of his belongings, I stayed downstairs in the offices until he left. I thought he would be giving me a hug, but he was too angry. After my experience, which stripped me of all my freedoms, I could only think about my survival. To be honest I hardly thought of Phillip during my three day, 72-hour stay in hell. I have seen the worst when it comes to humanity. Every nurse and doctor in there knew they were drugging the mentally ill when they didn't want to take the drugs. The psyche ward of Sarasota Memorial needs to be shut down. The Baker Act needs to be overturned. The movie should be released right before the election of 2020. The movie would reveal how corrupt the state of Florida really is.

In all my life, I have never met so many dumb, uneducated people as I have in the 18 months I have lived in this awful state. Yes, Florida may be home to the grandmas and grandpas, but also the rednecks and the smoking uneducated hicks. That is why I have referred to this state as *Floriduh*. These people, as a group, are the stupidest most uneducated people I have ever met.

I am applying for my full medical report about my awful experience. I have called the Florida bar and several independent malpractice lawyers. None would take my case. I decided to go to the local FBI office to tell them my story. I did and I never got a call back. Donald Trump's picture was in the office of the FBI. I wondered how he would feel to know what I knew. The FBI never called me back. All the lawyers I contacted in Florida said they were sorry about what I went through, but they couldn't help me. I reached out to my friend in New York and told him I wanted to file a class-action case against the state of Florida, and everyone employed surrounding the Baker Act in Florida. I was surprised that the FBI never got back to me. I reached out to many reporters and news sources about my story, and no one cared. Johnson and Johnson have DEEP pockets. I have not and will never give up on telling this story. I promised the woman who I met there I would try to help them.

They all left that day with me. They didn't go home; they went upstairs to the extended stay mental institution where they continually drug patients indefinitely. If my three-day bill was $12,000 and change then what do you think a three-month extended stay would cost? Who do you think pays for these patients? The federal government does. The state of Florida is getting off scot-free. Is knowledge really power all the time? I wonder.

I understand now why everyone who lives in Florida talks about the weather all the time. The weather is the only redeeming feature about residing in the state—and the no state income tax. Florida should pay people to live there from my experiential point of view. I am out of here as fast as humanly possible. It is time for me to go back to where I am from. I have always been in a 'New York state of mind' thanks to one of my favorites, Billy Joel. The big apple has always been and always will be a big part of my heart and soul. I don't care if it is the most expensive place to live in the world. I am financially climbing my way back. One day soon I will reach the rainbow and my pot of gold will be there. I am reminded now of what my dad always asked me repeatedly for the last decade, "Terri, when are you going to save for a rainy day?"

My answer has been consistently the same, "Dad, this is the rainy day."

Chapter 7

"When We Live in the Experience of Our Knowledge, Our Past Journey, We Have Reached the Pinnacle of Leadership." – Terri Rogers

It is December 10, 2019. What a day! What are the odds? At approximately 5:00 pm, on the corner of West 33rd and 8th Ave, coming back from a *NOoodle* meeting, I was hungry. I decided to walk 15 blocks out of my way to get a couple of slices from my favorite pizza place, La Suprema Pizza. The best slice of spinach pizza in the world. I overhear a man talking on his cell phone. I knew that voice! I turned around and it was Kevin O'Leary, Mr. Wonderful from "Shark Tank."

I waited until he was off the phone and then with a big smile I said, "Kevin, Terri Rogers."

He said, "Have we met?"

I said, "Yes!"

He said, "Where…when?"

I said, "Shark Tank 2013."

He said, "Remind me of the company again?"

I said, "*NOoodle*, noodle with an extra O.com."

He said, "Oh, yeah, what happened again?"

I said, "At the time, we had an unethical multibillion dollar company House Foods Japan dba House Foods USA. pretending to be our co-packer. They even built a phony manufacturing line they showed me in their factory in Garden Grove. The lying greedy men running this company never made one bag of NOoodle. They were just a greedy middleman company using me to create the market for them." He said smiling back at me. "How did it go?"

I said, "Not great. I went bankrupt in 2015 and then suffered two detached retinas."

He said, "It's not easy being an entrepreneur."

I nodded in agreement and then I asked him, "Kevin why don't you tell them the truth about the show?"

Then his body language completely changed, he clearly was uncomfortable with my request to him, and he said, "It is true. We have made a lot of people millionaires."

I said, "Yes and what about all the other people like me?"

He said with an awkward smile, "Sorry, shit happens."

The light turned green, and we both walked in separate directions. I walked into Penn Station to take the No. 1 train home. Did that just happen? Yes, it really did.

In the month of May 2020, I spent most of my time cooking for the front lines at Mt. Sinai. A company called Kettle Creations and I teamed up and we donated many *NOoodle* Pho Soups. I baked brownies for the workers at my local Chase. I made cereal bars for the workers at my Duane Reade. I wanted to prove to everyone selling those cereals they were completely full of sugar by using them as a base. I also worked on getting new doctors. I needed an internist. I needed a new gynecologist and I needed to see doctors to address why I lost my mind starting March 1st, 2020.

Due to corona, the gynecologist was the only doctor who would see me. It was over a year that I last saw my negligent gynecologist in Sarasota. I needed my one-year pap smear. Prior to being committed illegally in May 2019 into Sarasota Memorial Hospital (Bayside Wing), I had just seen my new doctor. My mom referred her to me, her name is Dr. Manual, she was very nice.

At the time, I was showing signs of premenopausal symptoms and she was testing my blood to see my levels. This was a follow up visit; she was to remove my second Merina IUD (I had two back-to-back for a total of ten years in my body). She said she couldn't give me a good diagnosis of entering menopause until the Merina IUD was removed. She took it out that day, it was May 23rd, 2019. She held it up and said, "Here it is"! It was huge! I couldn't believe I had that thing in me for ten years, the second one of two. It is a form of birth control, and it also can stop certain negative occurrences in women's bodies. Dr. Manuel never said a word about what I was to expect. Now that she took the Merina IUD out of my body, I was no longer producing any progesterone. Why didn't she tell me? Why didn't she help me, and my body stabilize during this severe transition?

In 2007, I had been diagnosed with 'cystic breasts and ovaries.' I had been hospitalized twice for a cist erupting during my period. The first ER doctor diagnosed me with gonorrhea, I was 25 years old. The following day my gyno reminded me to call her first even if it was in the middle of the night. She did an ultrasound and confirmed what she already knew. I didn't have gonorrhea. Good thing because my then fiancé was thinking of calling off our wedding. The second time it happened I was 38 years old. I was driving to see a customer and I got shooting pains while I was driving. I pulled over and called an ambulance. I was there for two days in excruciating pain. It was awful. At first my ER doctors thought I had appendicitis. They were working on scheduling surgery but first they wanted the gynecologist on duty to look. Sure enough, it was another cyst eruption. The next week my gynecologist Lori Decker recommended an IUD. She explained it would prevent me from having my period. She said I would still have hormonal imbalances; the blood would be prevented from flowing which will ensure that you don't ever experience a cist erupting.

After five years, it was working great! I was always a monogamist, a serial monogamist. I loved that I didn't have to worry about getting pregnant *and* ever having a cyst erupt again. My doctor told me It was time to take out the old *IUD* and put a new one it. She said they only work for five years. This time she had me sign some paperwork. To be honest I didn't read the paperwork, I just signed it. I trusted my doctor. She never told me of the potential side effects, i.e. I may go blind and then lose my mind. If she would have told me the new evidence instead of handing me a multi-page contract while I was in stirrups I would have declined. I would have taken my chances on a third ovarian cyst exploding. I would know it was a cist and it wouldn't be as scary. The pain does eventually go away after a few days. When I owned a catering company some of my best customers were pharmaceutical companies. I was always wondering why they would spend hundreds and thousands of dollars on gourmet lunches for the doctor offices. Now I understand why. Gourmet daily lunches for the entire office is a big perk for everyone who works there. Perks to customers I have learned come in many forms. They can be cash spiffs, free vacations, free lunches, etc., etc. Rationalize it anyway you want but from where I sit, they are all bribes.

I always want to find the answers to problems. I am a truth seeker. A couple of months after my Baker Act, I started to wonder what happened to me. I was extremely edgy prior during Memorial Day. I started to be disgusted by everyone I loved. It wasn't until August 2019 that I remembered right before I got hospitalized, I had my second Merina IUD taken out. I started googling and googling and googling. I finally had the answer I was looking for. I finally understood why at the end of May I started having headaches. I started having constant ringing in my ears. I was not able to sleep, and I felt as if my brain was on speed. My brain was not able to relax. *OMG! WOW!* I thought, *it is sooo true*, *#wedontknowwhatwedontknow.*

Mirena lawsuits claim the birth control device causes serious side effects. One of the side effects is it deteriorates retinas. The intrauterine device (IUD) has migrated, perforating the uterus in some cases. The IUD has also been linked to increased pressure in the brain. At least 2,700 women have sued Bayer over these adverse events. Some of these cases settled in 2018 for $2.2 million.

Why Women Are Filing Mirena Lawsuits

Mirena lawsuits stem from the device's *severe side effects*. In early 2018, Bayer announced a settlement that resolved thousands of Mirena-related lawsuits. The settlement only included claims related to IUD migration and perforation.

However, many women have sued Bayer due to a serious condition known as pseudotumor cerebri ("false tumor"). This condition can cause tumor-like symptoms in the brain. Bayer's 2018 settlement did not settle any cases related to pseudotumor cerebri. *These cases are still pending.*

Mirena Side Effects Claimed in Lawsuits

- Device migration
- Device embedment
- Organ perforation
- *Pseudotumor cerebri*
- *Ectopic pregnancy*

Pseudotumor Cerebri /Idiopathic Intracranial Hypertension

Pseudotumor cerebri (PTC) is a buildup of pressure in the brain. It is also known as idiopathic intracranial hypertension (IIH).

Increased pressure can exert force on the brain, leading to several symptoms like a brain tumor. These can include vision changes, balance issues, and mental or memory problems.

PTC can happen to anyone, but certain medications can increase the risk. Among those drugs is levonorgestrel. Levonorgestrel is the progestin-based hormone used in Mirena. A *2015 study by Canadian researchers* demonstrated this effect. In the study, women who used Mirena were more likely to develop PTC than women who did not use Mirena.

Women who have experienced PTC while using a Mirena IUD could be eligible for compensation.

- Vision changes (e.g., double vision, loss of vision, etc.)
- Dizziness
- Headaches
- Nausea
- Vomiting
- Depression
- Neck stiffness
- Difficulty walking
- Tinnitus (ringing in the ears)
- Memory problems

Ectopic Pregnancy

An ectopic pregnancy occurs when a fertilized egg attaches to a structure outside the uterus. Most ectopic pregnancies occur in the fallopian tube, the structure connecting the uterus to the ovary.

This type of pregnancy can cause life-threatening complications like bleeding and fallopian tube rupture. More than 1,200 ectopic pregnancies have been reported by Mirena users.

FDA Warnings About Mirena IUD Marketing

In April 2009, the FDA warned Bayer and the public about the company's misleading Mirena marketing. Mirena should only be used for up to five years before replacement. However, Bayer's marketing did not include this information. Instead, the initial marketing implied the IUD could be used indefinitely. Bayer also failed to state that Mirena was primarily recommended for women who already had at least one child.

Note: Bayer submitted a Supplemental New Drug Application (NDA) for Mirena in October 2019. The NDA seeks to extend Mirena's labeling to allow use up to six years. As of July 2020, the NDA is still underway. Mirena is currently approved for only five years of use.

The FDA's Adverse Events Reporting System (FAERS) keeps track of device injuries. As of July 2020, FAERS includes 104,000 *reports concerning Mirena.* Motivated by these injuries, thousands of women have filed lawsuits against Bayer. Many of these women make similar legal complaints. Specific allegations claim Bayer:

- Designed, produced, and knowingly sold a defective product
- Failed to research and warn the public about dangerous side effects
- Concealed the dangerous side effects
- Engaged in false and misleading marketing
- Misrepresented the benefits of the device
- Breached implied and express warranty

- Failed to issue a recall once the information came to light about the complications

Mirena Multidistrict and Multicounty Litigation

Bayer has settled thousands of Mirena lawsuits. But there are still some cases pending. Many individual Mirena lawsuits have been consolidated into federal *multidistrict litigation (MDL)*. Others have been consolidated into multicounty litigation (MCL) in state courts. There are currently three sets of mass torts covering Mirena IUDs:

- MDL 2434 in United States District Court
- MDL 2767 in United States District Court
- NJ MCL 297 in New Jersey State Courts

MDL 2767: Mirena Pseudotumor Cerebri

Many women have experienced complications due to a buildup of pressure in the brain. This is known as *pseudotumor cerebri (PTC)*. This condition has symptoms like a brain tumor. Research studies have linked the hormone in the Mirena IUD with this dangerous condition.

In April 2017, the U.S. Judicial Panel on Multidistrict Litigation (JPML) consolidated all Mirena PTC lawsuits. They formed MDL 2767 in the Southern District of New York. This included 113 pending Mirena cases in 17 districts and 37 potential actions. As of July 2020, more than 900 cases had been filed in this MDL.

MDL 2434: Mirena Migration, Perforation and Embedment

In June 2013, the JPML consolidated many Mirena IUD lawsuits into an MDL in the Southern District of New York. These cases claim complications due to:

- Device migration
- Organ perforation
- Device embedment

The MDL argued Mirena's initial label did not contain warnings about secondary perforation. The label in question was used from 2008 through 2014. It did state that Mirena IUD perforation may occur during insertion and escape detection until sometime later. But claimants said the contraceptive device could cause perforation at any time.

Most of these cases were settled in April 2018.

New Jersey MCL 297

Many plaintiffs in New Jersey made similar allegations to those in the New York MDL. So, the NJ Supreme Court consolidated cases in multicounty litigation (MCL) in 2013.

In April 2018, Judge Rachelle Harz appointed a Special Master. The Special Master would oversee settlement negotiations between Bayer and plaintiffs in MCL 297. Garretson Resolution Group was appointed in June 2018 as the lien resolution administrator. This settlement was part of the 4,100-case settlement announced by Bayer in April 2018.

Individual Mirena IUD Lawsuits

The first Mirena IUD lawsuits generally concerned device migration. Below is a summary of complications experienced by some of the earliest claimants:

Desaree Nicole Lee Johnson suffered pain when her Mirena IUD perforated her uterus and moved into her abdomen. After undergoing surgery to remove it, she became pregnant. She then experienced vaginal bleeding and had a miscarriage. She claims Bayer knowingly released an unsafe and defective product. She also says their actions directly lead to her injuries.

Melody Williams began experiencing severe pain and abdominal cramping. It had been less than a year since her Mirena IUD was implanted. As a result, Williams required surgical removal of the device. The first removal failed. Surgeons attempted a second procedure and found the IUD had migrated through her fallopian tube. Williams experienced pain, distress, and numerous medical procedures because of the IUD. She and her husband filed a suit accusing Bayer of negligence and reckless disregard for public safety.

Mirena Lawsuit Settlement Amounts

In April 2018, Bayer signed an agreement to settle approximately 4,000 Mirena lawsuits. The settlement related to claims of perforations caused by the IUD. The settlement includes cases in federal MDL 2434 and NJ MCL 297. It also included cases filed in St. Louis City Circuit Court (Missouri) and all pending cases in California.

The total settlement amount was $12.2 million. But individual settlement amounts for Mirena lawsuits vary depending on the details of each individual case.

This settlement only resolved cases related to perforation by the Mirena device. Other claims related to ectopic pregnancy and idiopathic intracranial hypertension (ITC) are still outstanding.

Mirena Lawsuit FAQs

Can I File a Mirena Lawsuit?

Women who received a Mirena IUD implant and experienced one of the following severe side effects may be eligible for compensation (*legal damages*):

- Perforation of the uterus or another organ
- Migration of the device
- Intense cranial pressure or headaches—idiopathic intracranial hypertension (ITC) or pseudotumor cerebri (PTC)
- Unintended pregnancies
- Ectopic pregnancies or other pregnancy complications

How Much Is the Mirena Lawsuit Individual Settlement Amount?

The Mirena settlement announced in April 2018 covered about 4,000 perforation cases. The total settlement amount announced in Bayer's financial filings was $12.2 million. This amounts to about $3,050 per person. However, the exact amount will differ based on the final number of plaintiffs who agree to the settlement. Adjustments may also be made based on the severity of everyone's case.

Additional settlements could be reached for other outstanding cases. This may include plaintiffs who choose not to sign onto the April 2018 settlement. If your Mirena IUD caused a serious side effect, you should consider starting legal action. Don't wait because each state has its own deadline (*statute of limitations*).

What Does a Mirena Lawyer Cost?

Mirena lawsuits, like *other medical device lawsuits*, are filed on what is known as a contingency basis. This means that you will not have to pay anything up front. Instead, you will only pay legal fees if you win money for your claim either through a verdict or settlement.

Authored by

Curtis Weyant

Contributor

Curtis Weyant has more than 20 years as a writer, editor, and communicator, publishing on a wide variety of topics, especially in the financial, legal, and medical fields. At ConsumerSafety.org, Curtis managed the day-to-day publication of all content from 2016-2019.

Sources

1   Alder JB, Fraunfelder FT, Edwards R. Levonorgestrel Implants and Intracranial Hypertension. *The New England Journal of Medicine.* 1995;332(25):1720-1. doi: 10.1056/NEJM199506223322519

2   Bayer. Legal Risks. *Interim Report: First Quarter 2018.* May 3, 2018.

3   Bayer HealthCare Pharmaceuticals. Drug Label Information: Mirena. July 2008.

4   Department of Neurology. Pseudotumor Cerebri. Columbia University.

5   Doshi S. Letter re: NDA No. 21-225 Mirena intrauterine system, from Department of Health and Human Services to Bayer Healthcare Pharmaceuticals, Inc. U.S. Food and Drug Administration. March 2009.

6   Etminan M, Luo H, Gustafson P. Risk of intracranial hypertension with intrauterine levonorgestrel. *Therapeutic Advances in Drug Safety.* May 25, 2015;6(3):110-113. doi: 10.1177/2042098615588084

7   Grant GA. Notice to the Bar: Mass Torts –
    Application for Centralized Management
    (Multicounty Litigation) of New Jersey State-Court
    Litigation Involving Mirena Contraceptive Device.
    New Jersey Courts. August 13, 2012.

8   Harz RL. In Re Mirena Litigation. Superior Court
    of New Jersey Law Division: Bergen County. Case
    No. 297 Master Docket No. BER-L-4098-13 MCL.
    April 10, 2018.

9   Lexis Legal News. Bayer, Plaintiffs Say They've
    Agreed to Settle Mirena IUD Perforation Claims.
    Law360. August 14, 2018.

10 New Jersey Courts. Mirena.

11 Sieniuc K. Wipeout of Mirena MDL to Be
    Challenged At 2nd Circ. *Law360*. August 19, 2016.

12 Vratil KH. Transfer Order. *In Re: Mirena IUD
    Products Liability Litigation. July 28, 2016. United
    States District Court Southern District of New
    York, MDL No. 2434.* U.S. Judicial Panel on
    Multidistrict Litigation. April 8, 2013. Case 7:13-
    mc-02434-CS-LMS.

13 Willet G. NDA Clinical Review: Mirena
    (Levonorgestrel-releasing intrauterine system).
    U.S. Food and Drug Administration. March 6,
    2009.

After days of trying to get a lawyer to take my case I
was told I had no case. I had no case because I signed the
paperwork with the second IUD. It was after the warnings
came out. I was always gullible and believed everything

people told me, especially people in authority, i.e., my doctors

I remember always being very sensitive to drugs. During my many surgeries the pain pills, although necessary, made me have hot flashes. I took mushrooms once when I was at UOFA in Tucson, they didn't agree with me. I took acid once in college at a dead show. It was the worst experience of my life. Xanax made me sleep for days. Cocaine made me wired, nothing else mattered but having more Cocaine. I had ecstasy once in Ibiza, Spain when I was 21. I had so much fun that I swore I would never do it again. I knew it must have been terrible for my body. I was grateful for the experience. I was always a person to try new things. I loved that about life. I also knew for me at fifty the only drug that was good for me and my psyche was cannabis, in moderation of course.

As a businesswoman who has spent most of my adult life cooking healthier food and living a healthy lifestyle, I was against taking drugs for myself except for cannibus, coffee, and alcohol. I also had to watch the way I took cannabis because smoking stirs up my allergies. I had learned that I have a very sensitive body. Even if I have one more than two martinis, I could be sick in bed for the next twenty-four hours with a terrible hangover.

In June 2020, I had a false-positive pap smear, which led to a biopsy which thankfully was negative. I expressed my concerns to my new Gynecologist in NYC regarding my Merina IUD pseudo cerebri brain tumor, he marked my chart. I was able to speak to the social worker Julie on duty. We spoke for 45 minutes, and I told her my recent history. I tried to recount exactly what I went through over the last couple of months. During my appointments, I was adamant with my doctors I did not want to go on any drugs to alter my brain. They agreed, we needed more answers.

I started to spend more and more time in Central Park. My factory was back up and running. I was ready to get back to work. I focused on getting my website up and running. I created new social media platforms. I knew my business over the years had created a form of stress that triggered my allergies. I didn't think of my allergies much, I guess because I was feeling better. Again, I was completely out of my singular. The epi-pens I had in my possession from my urgent care visit in February were just recalled. I still didn't have an internist; they were not taking new appointments due to covid. I decided to go back to the Urgent care on Columbus Ave.

The cute young doctor came in. I said, "Hi!" and I started to explain to her what I went thru the last three months. I told her I lost my mind in March/April. I thought the movies I was watching were talking to me. I was going to a big Party with Kobe and Vanessa Bryant. She said, "Terri...you must be allergic to steroids, I will note your chart."

"How did you know I took steroids?" I asked bewildered.

She said, "I was the ER doctor that prescribed them to you at the end of February."

I looked at her and said, "I don't recognize you."

She said with a big smile, "I was nine months pregnant when we met, and I prescribed you the steroids. I had my baby a couple of months ago, I look different now than I did then. You're allergic to steroids. I will mark your chart now."

"Why didn't you google it when you were going through it?" she asked.

I was staring up at her stunned. After a long pause I said, "I must have forgotten I took them."
Steroidal psychosis – Steroidal psychosis
nawo.online
*Search for Steroidal **psychosis**. Search more about the symptom, causes and treatment of Mental Illness.*

- Some prescription drugs like steroids and stimulants can also cause symptoms of psychosis. People who have an addition to alcohol or certain drugs can experience psychotic symptoms if they suddenly stop drinking or taking those drugs. A head injury or an illness or infection that affects the brain can cause symptoms of psychosis.

Psychosis: Symptoms, Causes, and Risk Factors

www.healthline.com/health/psychosis#:
~:text=Some%20prescription%20drugs%20like%20
20steroids%20and%20stimulants%20can,
affects%20the%20brain%20can%20cause%20sy
mptoms%20of%20psychosis.

1. People also ask

Can steroids cause mania?

Can Solu Medrol cause psychosis?

Can testosterone cause psychosis?

Can prednisone cause psychosis?

effect of corticosteroid use and most commonly occurs at prednisone doses above 20mg/day given over a long period. 1 2 3 Roughly ten percent of patients remain psychotic after the steroid dose is decreased.

11. *Systemic Corticosteroid – Associated Psychiatric Adverse Effects*

12. *www.uspharmacist.com/article/systemic...Jul 14, 2016· Whenever possible, tapering corticosteroids—ideally to less than 40 mg daily— is recommended as a first step to manage corticosteroid-induced psychosis; tapering and discontinuation of steroids may be sufficient to improve psychiatric symptoms without requiring additional medications. 10*

13. *Psychiatric Adverse Effects of Corticosteroids*

14. www.mayoclinicproceedings.org/article/S002 5-6196...

15. Although disturbances of mood, cognition, sleep, and behavior as well as frank delirium or even psychosis are possible, the most common adverse effects of. short-term corticosteroid therapy are euphoria and hypomania. Conversely, long-term therapy tends to induce depressive symptoms.

16. *Steroids And Psychosis – Video Results*

Epilogue

My situation today is a situation that has arisen out of my duty to help the masses of people who are suffering as Americans. We have a huge choice to make today. Do we want to live into a future that resembles our past? When we try to bring the past into our future, all we get is more of the past. The past was not great, it was terrible when it comes to the health of our planet and our future grandchildren's potential life span. All I continue to hear is when we are going to get back to normal. Normal…we want to go back to normal? Not me, I didn't love the normal where the greedy got richer and the sweet hard-working people got poorer. Is it possible mother nature is God? Is it possible that Mother nature created this virus so humanity would be forced to do the work needed to save our planet? I say unequivocally…*yes!*

Little by little and day by day I am going to collect and form a group of powerful leaders who have the same vision as I do. I intend to one day turn my company, *NOoodle Inc.* into a B-corporation 100% for our children, GENamaZing. We manufacture and market plant-based foods. Fun fast and better for us foods, made in the USA. To be effective, I believe our team, the home team, needs to occupy the most powerful seat in the world. The president of the USA. Why vote for me for president? I would say it wouldn't be a vote for me, it would be a vote for US. Why us? It is only and all about us. Who is us? We are us. God is us. We are God. Mother nature is leading us to this place in the future because she is part of God too.

My answers are explained in the lyrics written by some of my favorite artists; First, sing the lyrics of a song written and recorded by Lady Gaga, *A million reasons.* Second, sing the lyrics of a song written and recorded by Pink, *What about US?* Third, sing the lyrics of a song written and performed by the Black-Eyed Peas, *where is the Love?* Fourth sing the lyrics of 'Glory' written by John Legend and Common. Fifth sing Justin's and Chance the Rappers lyrics in "Holy". Lastly sing the lyrics of a song by Kenny Loggins, *Conviction of the heart*, which is exactly what we all need now, conviction of the heart. The hands that rock the cradle should be the hands that rule the world. We are the mothers of dragons, and we are the breakers of chains.

"We will March forth in Love." – Chef Terri Rogers